Janina Scarlet is a licensed Clinical Psychologist and the award-wining author of *Superhero Therapy* as well as *Therapy Quest*, *Super-Women*, *Dark Agents*, *Harry Potter Therapy* and *Supernatural Therapy*. She has also contributed to the following books: *Star Wars Psychology*, *Walking Dead Psychology*, *Captain America vs. Iron Man Psychology*, *Game of Thrones Psychology*, *Star Trek Psychology* and *Doctor Who Psychology*. In addition, Dr Scarlet is an international workshop trainer in Superhero Therapy, having presented at international conferences, including ACBS, as well as numerous popular culture conventions, in training mental health professionals in using Superhero Therapy.

Dr Scarlet received training in ACT by ACT creators Steve Hayes, Kelly Wilson and Kirk Strosahl, with Dr Hayes having endorsed her first two books with Little, Brown. Dr Scarlet is frequently interviewed about her work and has been featured on the BBC, CBS, MTV News, CW, *Huffington Post* and others. She is also frequently invited to speak at pop culture conferences, including the San Diego Comic Con, London Comic Con and others, and has been providing training and consulting internationally. She is the recipient of the Eleanor Roosevelt Human Rights Award by the United Nations Association for her work on Superhero Therapy.

Praise for *It Shouldn't Be This Way*

'This extremely well-written book grabs you from the first pages and walks you through the challenges of some of life's most painful moments. It addresses that core question that all of us fear, but may not even realise is there, looming over us, until life happens: what will we do when nothing we do will do? Here's the beginning of an answer: read this gentle, strong and very wise book'

Steven C. Hayes, Ph.D., originator of Acceptance and Commitment Therapy and author of *A Liberated Mind: How to Pivot Toward What Matters*

Also by Janina Scarlet

Superhero Therapy

Therapy Quest

Dark Agents

Harry Potter Therapy

Super-Women

Super Survivors

It Shouldn't Be This Way:

Learning to Accept the Things You Just Can't Change

Janina Scarlet, Ph.D.

ROBINSON

ROBINSON

First published in Great Britain in 2021 by Robinson

3 5 7 9 10 8 6 4

Important Note
This book is not intended as a substitute for medical advice or treatment.
Any person with a condition requiring medical attention should
consult a qualified medical practitioner or suitable therapist.

A CIP catalogue record for this book
is available from the British Library.

ISBN: 978-1-47214-598-7

Typeset in Gentium by Initial Typesetting Services, Edinburgh
Printed and bound in Great Britain by Clays Ltd, Elcograf S.p.A.

Papers used by Robinson are from well-managed forests
and other responsible sources.

Robinson
An imprint of
Little, Brown Book Group
Carmelite House
50 Victoria Embankment
London EC4Y 0DZ

An Hachette UK Company
www.hachette.co.uk

www.littlebrown.co.uk

To anyone whose heart has ever bled with agony,
to anyone who has ever wished things to be different,
to anyone who has ever felt weak when they were actually strong, and
to anyone who was ever shamed into silencing their inner suffering.

Contents

Introduction   1

PART I:
Acceptance, Avoidance, and Everything in Between: The Why and the What

1. Paul   7
2. Ambiguous Losses   11
3. Feeling Stuck   27
4. The Way Out   37
5. Avoidance   45
6. Origin Story   55
7. Acceptance vs Enabling   63
8. Resistance and Fire   69
9. What It Brings Up   79
10. No Regrets   93

PART II:
Acceptance in Practice: The How

11. Gentle Acceptance Practices   101
12. The Core of the Onion   113
13. Empathic Distress and Coping With Social Injustice   123

It Shouldn't Be This Way

14.	Acceptance of Assistance	137
15.	Building Boundaries	147
16.	Finding YOUR Voice	163
17.	Overcoming Obstacles and Setbacks	167
18.	Your Phoenix Moment	177

References	181
Resources	187
Acknowledgements	189
Index	191

Introduction

There are no manuals on how to be a human being, no official manuals anyway. Most of us are stuck figuring out how to navigate this adventure we call *life*, often with little guidance. Some of us might have been met with harsh judgement, stigma or criticism when we might have tried to seek help or support from others.

Worse, sometimes we might see other people seemingly 'having it all together', and all the while we might be struggling just to get out of bed in the morning. We might assume that we are the only ones going through a hard time. We might also erroneously assume that going through depression, anxiety, trauma or any other mental or physical struggle means that we are 'weak'. The truth is, however, that suffering is not a weakness, it is a foundation upon which you can discover your inner strength.

I am a licensed clinical psychologist and my biggest passion is helping people learn different ways of managing their mental health struggles. As someone who was frequently told of the need to 'be strong' as a way of being shamed out of feeling anxious or depressed, I have learned first-hand about the damaging effects of emotion suppression and how such emotional avoidance can lead to a significant worsening of symptoms.

In my work with my clients, I utilise an intervention called acceptance and commitment therapy (ACT). ACT focuses on learning to mindfully accept things that might be out of our control while living a meaningful life based on our deepest core values.[1] This intervention has been shown to be helpful for treating depression, anxiety disorders, PTSD, chronic pain and other chronic illnesses, addiction, as well as many other disorders.[2]

What is acceptance?

At the core of ACT is the acceptance skill. Many people might be told that they have to suppress and avoid their emotions and 'focus on the positive'. Acceptance refers to the willingness to face and process the emotions and the events in our lives that we cannot change. For example, acceptance might refer to the willingness to process the pain of a past trauma or the anxiety about an uncertain future if it means living a full and meaningful life. Acceptance might also mean being true to yourself instead of conforming to outdated and absurd societal expectations. Acceptance is essentially a method of self-empowerment and self-exploration.

Getting the most out of this book

This book is broken up into two parts. In the first part, we will go over what acceptance is and what it is not, as well as why it is

1 Hayes, et al. (2011).
2 Dindo, et al. (2017).

important. I will also discuss my experiences with acceptance practices, as well as clinical examples of other individuals who have struggled with acceptance and their subsequent acceptance journeys.

The second part of the book focuses on how to practise acceptance. In this part, you will learn specific acceptance exercises, as well as how to manage some of the possible challenges that might come up along the way.

In order to get the most out of this book, it might be most helpful to read one or two chapters per week to take time to process the material you are reading. Some people find it helpful to use a notebook or a journal to write down their thoughts while reading about and practising the different exercises in this book. In addition, some people find it helpful to read a book like this when they are by themselves, whereas others prefer to read it with a book club or with their therapist. Many people benefit from discussing what the various chapters have brought up for them or journaling about their reflections.

In a world where most of us feel the impossible pressure to conform to everyone else's expectations, allow this one journey to be your own. You are allowed your feelings and your experiences and you are allowed to go at your own speed. Breathe. Take the pressure off. Thank you for being wonderful.

PART I:

Acceptance, Avoidance and Everything in Between: The Why and the What

PART I.

Chapter 1
Paul

The first thing I remember thinking when I met Paul was, 'Wow, he's *dreamy*.' The second thing I thought was, 'He's probably full of himself.'

I was fifteen and Paul was a blind date, pushed on me by one of my classmates who prided herself on being the school's unofficial matchmaker. Paul was seventeen and already in college, having graduated school the year prior. He was brilliant.

I hated him.

At least for a moment.

His hair was chin length and neat. He wore a navy-blue button-up shirt under his black leather jacket and his jeans looked like they were sewn around him. His high cheekbones made him look both handsome and distinguished.

He looked at me in that disarming way that someone *really* looks at you, as if there is no one else in that moment or that universe. He smiled, and my heart leapt as I dropped my trigonometry book. We both bent down to pick it up and our eyes met once again.

I smiled hoping that he didn't see me blushing. He returned my smile and picked up my book without ever taking his eyes off me. He offered his hand to help me stand up, which was good because I was already falling in every sense of that word.

7

'You're from Ukraine, right?' His eyes were looking directly into mine. Tiny wrinkles formed around his eyes every time he smiled, and I found myself smiling again.

'Yes.'

'How was it living there? It must have been hard. I heard that even years after World War II, people are still affected, even to this day.'

His gentle enquiry, full of consideration and compassion, brought tears to my eyes. 'It was . . . not easy.'

'I can imagine. I'm actually studying Russian history now at my university.'

My judgements washed away with each new thing I discovered about him. I learned that he and his family immigrated to the United States from Greece when he was a small child. I saw that behind the navy-blue shirt was the palette of an artist. Underneath the neatly combed hair was a brilliant mind that shared my love of history. Underneath the tough leather jacket was a guy whose family experienced much struggle when they immigrated from another country, as did mine.

It took us four hours to walk six blocks, a walk that led into a year of a movie-like romance. My family was resistant at first. Coming from a traditional Jewish family, my parents were not keen to allow me to date a Greek Orthodox college boy. But over time, his smile won over my family, too. He was invited to family events – birthdays, holidays and weddings.

Two days before my brother's wedding, Paul and his father had to fly out to Florida for a family emergency. 'I'll call you when I get there. I love you,' were the last words he said to me.

Paul

His sister's call came a few days later, 'Paul got hit by a car . . . he's dead . . . I'm so sorry.'

As I hung up the phone, I slid down the wall, my heart beating 500 miles a minute, trying to escape to another world, the one where he still existed. One where I could still feel his always-chilly hands in mine. One where I could feel his heartbeat when I lay my head upon his chest.

I felt numb. I felt gutted . . . but more than that. I felt like there was no me left. The world felt too big. Empty. Too empty to be allowed.

In the world outside, the smiling people enjoying their winter holidays just somehow seemed like they weren't aware.

I remember thinking, *How can they be so happy at a time like this? Don't they know I'm dying? Don't they know that he's dead?*

I wanted to scream but no sound would come.

The next few days were a blur. My brother called from his honeymoon. I don't remember talking to him, but I know that I did. My parents, my *Jewish* parents, took me to a Greek Orthodox church so I could honour Paul's memory in my own way.

My body felt both heavy and empty. My gut felt like I'd been punched repeatedly. I kept staring at the ceiling at a crack shaped like a butterfly, wishing that I could find the courage to die. I called Paul's sister twice to check on her, the only phone calls I could find the strength to make. She cried both times that I was able to reach her. She said that it was too difficult for her to talk about what happened. When we would hang up the phone, I would feel even more useless and broken than before.

Returning to school several weeks later, I felt like I was in some kind of a cruel dream. Nothing seemed real. Everything was a fog, torn between one reality and the next. I moved in slow motion, as if in an independent film where everything around me was moving at triple speed. When I got to my literature class, I could feel the last of my energy drain as I collapsed into my seat.

'Where have YOU been?' Kelly's raspy voice came from behind me.

I turned around slowly, weighing out how best to tell her. She knew Paul but I wasn't sure if she knew what happened to him. 'Paul went to Florida over the winter holidays. He was hit by a car . . . he died,' I said, trying to push down the heavy lump in my throat.

Kelly looked at me with her head to the side, looking both surprised and confused.

After a few moments of pondering this, she said, 'Umm . . . no, he didn't. I just saw him yesterday on 5th Avenue. He was walking with his arm around some girl. His sister and her boyfriend were with them too. I just assumed you two broke up. I was going to call about it actually.'

Chapter 2
Ambiguous Losses

To this day, I still don't know which felt worse in the moment – thinking that my first boyfriend had died or finding out that he and his sister devised a dubious plan to fake his death in order for him to date his sister's best friend. Both felt like I was suffocating, drowning in a river that no one else could see. My lungs hurt from sobbing and, for more than two years afterward, I had little interest in any activity.

Over the following six months, my grades suffered. I went from an A student to barely a C student because doing my homework felt like running up a mountain with a backpack of boulders pulling on my chest.

When I believed that Paul was dead, everyone around me – my family and my close friends – supported me and checked up on me. I was grieving and I was also *allowed* to grieve.

When I learned that his supposed death was a lie, I still grieved but I wasn't sure why. I grieved the relationship that we no longer had. I grieved having him in my life. I grieved the person I was before. But I couldn't understand it.

When I told my close friends and family what he had done, their empathy quickly turned to anger, not only toward him, but also toward me.

'Just get over him. He doesn't deserve your tears.'

'What are you crying about? He's not even dead.'

'So what? People break up. Just get over it already!'

Their comments did not help. In fact, they only made me feel more alone in my pain. I didn't know back then that we can go through grief even when someone has not died. We can grieve a change in our relationship, a change in our ability, a loss of a job, a loss of a friendship, a loved one struggling with addiction or another type of an illness, all of which can feel like a part of us died. This kind of a loss is called an *ambiguous loss.*

An ambiguous loss is one that occurs 'in the in between' (for example, in between illness and death, or between heartbreak and disconnection), therefore not allowing the individual to have the kind of a closure that they might need in order to heal.[1] An ambiguous loss is also thought to be one of the most stressful types of losses, specifically because it defies the commonly understood definitions of grief and therefore does not always allow for the customary mourning and healing rituals. Because of this fact, we may struggle with processing our grief – unable to make sense of it, unable to take meaning from it and, therefore, unable to heal from it.[2] In other words, we grieve not only when someone dies but also when it feels like we are dying. And the more alone we feel in our grief, in the fog of confusion that such a loss brings, the louder and the more intense this loss might become.

Research related to ambiguous loss isn't new. It began in the late 1980s and has included families affected by wars, especially when family members were missing in action. It has also

1 Boss (2006).
2 Boss (2006).

included people who suddenly developed chronic illness or a disability, as well as people who experienced natural disasters, job loss or the loss of an opportunity. Other types of ambiguous losses include going through a divorce, uncovering an affair or another form of a deceit,[3] as well as experiencing a miscarriage, infertility or immigration.[4]

Some ambiguous losses can be placed in one of two categories. In the first category, someone might suddenly become physically absent (such as in the case of missing persons, ghosting or other types of physical disappearance). In the second category, a person might be physically present but psychologically absent. For example, the second type of an ambiguous loss can occur if our friend, parent or partner is abusive or emotionally unavailable to us.

Some people might experience this kind of a loss when there is a change in their relationship; for example, when a loved one develops a serious illness such as cancer, Alzheimer's disease, addiction or severe depression.[5] Other examples include changing where we live and with whom we might live, such as when people go through a breakup or a divorce.[6] Children who go through a larger amount of foster placements are more likely to have symptoms of post-traumatic stress disorder (PTSD) and ambiguous grief than children with fewer foster placements.[7]

3 Boss (2006).
4 Betz & Thorngren (2006).
5 Boss (2006).
6 Benson (2006).
7 Benson (2006).

Ambiguous losses may involve a person, an object, an experience or an event.[8] For example, in cases of child abductions, families might spend years searching for their children, not knowing whether to grieve or even *how* to grieve over the missing child, often blaming themselves; feeling too stuck to move on. In cases of miscarriage or infertility, the ambiguous losses might make it challenging to grieve. In these situations, it might be triggering to answer questions pertaining to the miscarriage or fertility issue, such as how many children a person has or when they should try to have children again.[9]

Sadly, many people might fail to understand how to support someone when they are going through a traumatic loss of any kind, especially an ambiguous one. Some individuals might offer poor advice, such as 'try to focus on the positive', or 'you need to move on from this', or 'at least you have your health'. Even when the person saying things like this to us might be well-meaning, what we might perceive is, 'I am not allowed to have my feelings', 'my feelings are unacceptable', or 'I am not allowed to express my feelings to others'.

Unfortunately, this can lead the person who is grieving to feel even more alone than they already do, while also feeling like a burden to others. The truth is that there is nothing anyone can say or do to take away the devastating and excruciating feelings of grief that we might be left with after a traumatic loss, including an ambiguous one. When people shame or criticise us into feeling differently than we do, or when they push

8 Betz & Thorngren (2006).
9 Betz & Thorngren (2006).

us to stifle our grief, it tends to backfire. Grief might turn into clinical depression or PTSD, leading some to substance abuse or other self-destructive behaviours, not because they want to destroy their lives, but because they never had the opportunity to properly process their pain.

Many of us might have been raised to believe that we should be able to control what we do, how we think, how we feel and what happens to us. This belief is called *the illusion of control.* In some situations, we might be able to control certain things. For example, you might have the control over what you wear, whether or not you eat breakfast, and how much information you might choose to share with someone. However, the illusion of control implies that we *should* be able to control everything that happens to us, as well as everything we think and feel. Unfortunately, having the illusion of control and then finding ourselves not being able to control aversive or painful outcomes can potentially lead to PTSD, depression or other mental health struggles.[10]

As a result of not being able to control what happened to us or how it made us feel, we might start shaming ourselves. In fact, we might be shaming ourselves just for the mere fact that we are having a painful emotion. Some refer to this as 'feeling bad for feeling bad'. I personally don't like to prescribe labels of 'good' or 'bad' to our emotions since I believe all are important and necessary. However, the essential result of the illusion of control is that we might emotionally beat ourselves up for

10 Hancock & Bryant (2020).

feeling down. For example, if you are feeling depressed, you might then say to yourself, 'What is wrong with you? Why can't you just get over it?'

This kind of emotionally abusive attitude toward ourselves is certainly not going to take away our grief or depression. Quite the opposite – it is more likely to intensify them, while also elevating our feelings of irritability, frustration and other negative emotions over time. It is for this reason that some people who experience depression might also be irritable, short-tempered and more argumentative with others – they are trying to suppress their emotional pain while also judging themselves for having this pain in the first place. As a result, people who are struggling with depression, anxiety or another challenge might end up lashing out at others or isolating from other people, right at the very time they are in the greatest need for compassion and support.

The illusion of control poses the assumption that we should be able to control everything that happens to us – that we should be able to do everything right in order to prevent any mistakes or bad things from happening. This line of thinking then implies that we are to blame for anything that goes wrong. In fact, when something bad happens, we might tear ourselves apart, thinking, 'If only I'd done something different, this wouldn't have happened.'

When someone dies suddenly, many of us might find ourselves wondering what we could have done differently to prevent their untimely death, sometimes blaming ourselves for this loss. When there is a tragic death in the family, some family members form private independent narratives about the tragedy being somehow their fault. Yet, most of the time, the family members might not share their narratives with one another, never realising that other members of their family likely blame themselves too. Family therapy can sometimes allow family members the opportunity to share how they understand their grief and which beliefs they might hold about what happened. In these situations, many people might be surprised to learn that other members of their family blame themselves as well. When this happens, many of us might be quick to defend others, reminding other people that the tragedy wasn't their fault. And in fact, having the ability to learn that other people might be having the same thoughts and experiences as we are, including the thoughts of self-blaming, can reduce some of our own shame and alienation that we might feel at that time.

In some instances, we might not only blame ourselves for a specific tragedy but also for our loss of ability. This is exactly what happened to one of the people I was working with in therapy a few years ago. Let's call him 'Chuck', although that is not his real name.

Chuck was a Marine, who witnessed a lot of death and destruction while on deployment. He lost several friends and blamed himself for their deaths. He was also injured in combat and was supposed to be in a wheelchair when he returned to the United States. However, Chuck was so ashamed of being in a wheelchair, that he refused it. He also refused the disability sticker for his car, saying that both the wheelchair and the car sticker should be reserved for the people who were 'truly disabled'.

Chuck was often 20–30 minutes late to his sessions because he had to park far away, rather than parking in the disabled spot. Instead of using the wheelchair, he elected to use two walking sticks, often falling over and re-injuring himself. By the time he would make it into my office, Chuck was in an enormous amount of pain. He would slump into his chair and tighten his lips from it.

He would look at the floor, his expression both blank and numb, as he would tell me about his injury, blaming himself for not being able to have prevented it somehow. When I asked him what he could have done differently, Chuck said, 'I shouldn't have gone out that day and I shouldn't have let my guys go, either.'

When I asked him why, he replied, 'I had a bad feeling that whole day, I should have listened to it.'

'Does the Marine Corps allow Marines to make judgement calls based on bad feelings?' I asked him.

He sighed and then shook his head. 'No, but . . . I just wish . . . I wish I did something . . . anything, you know, to stop it.'

It makes sense, of course. All of us wish things were different and often wish that we were able to prevent terrible things from happening. Under the illusion of control, we assume that so long as we do everything right, nothing bad will ever happen. Yet, this kind of thinking is a mind trap and will only lead to self-blame in situations in which, even if we did everything 'right', the bad outcome would likely have happened anyway.

It took a while for Chuck to begin to accept that there was nothing he could have done differently that day to prevent the deaths of his friends. But what he couldn't accept was his disability. He stated that his disability made him redefine himself. Prior to his injury, Chuck prided himself on being a 'superhero dad' and a 'superhero husband'. When I asked him what being a superhero meant to him, Chuck said that it meant being able to spend time with his family, including being able to run around with his little son in their backyard, and it meant being able to help his wife around the house. Because of his pain and his difficulty walking, Chuck avoided both of those types of activities. He felt so bad about himself, that he would hide out alone in his bedroom, believing himself to be 'weak' and 'broken'.

We talked about superheroes then and what it meant to be one. His belief was that superheroes were supposed to be 'strong', and always able to help others. I asked him if all superheroes needed to be able to walk in order to be strong and in order to be able to help others.

He looked up at me.

There was a long moment of silence between us.

He then said, 'Not all of them.'

He started naming superheroes who used wheelchairs, such as Charles Xavier from *X-Men*, Batgirl and others. They all had one thing in common – over time they learned to accept their being in a wheelchair, focusing on what they *could* do, as well as on what was *important* to them – helping other people.

The next session, Chuck was on time. He had a big smile on his face. And he was in a wheelchair.

He wheeled himself in and proclaimed, 'You won't believe how fast I am in this thing. I'm like the Flash!'

He told me that he chased his son around the backyard in a glorious game of tag and helped his wife with groceries.

He started making a list of jobs he was interested in once he was medically discharged from the military and a list of things he wanted to do in his spare time. Being able to accept this change in his ability liberated him to be able to focus on living his life, something he didn't think he would ever be able to do.

Whether it is a loss of a physical ability, loss of a house or a loss of a relationship, we might feel shattered. Broken. Shaken up to our very core. And it makes sense. How could we not feel that way? We are designed to feel, to belong and to have meaningful connections with others.[11] Our bodies respond positively when we interact with individuals we love and care about and respond painfully when we lose that level of connection.[12] The excruciating pain that we experience after a loss of any kind actually prompts us to be social and to seek social support.

When we have a conversation with a person we care about, when we are able to receive a hug or some notion of emotional support, our physical and emotional suffering might reduce.[13] This isn't a purely psychological experience. It is also a physiological one. When we are interacting with people (or non-human animals) that we care about, when we are either giving or receiving support from other people, our bodies secrete a special hormone called *oxytocin*. This hormone creates

11 Higa, et al. (2002); Kemp, et al. (2012); Xu & Roberts, (2010).
12 Coan, et al. (2006); Schimpff (2019).
13 Coan, et al. (2006); Kemp, et al. (2012).

the feelings of warmth and emotional safety in our body. We also know that oxytocin is actually responsible for our physical and emotional wellbeing. This hormone can regulate our heart, our nervous system, and is even thought to be involved in managing our lifespan.[14]

This means that when we lose a loved one in any capacity, either in a tragedy or due to a breakup or an illness, it makes sense that we would feel devastated. Even if the loved one is still alive, as might be the case with Alzheimer's disease or another illness in which an ongoing support from a loved one suddenly becomes unavailable, the feelings of loss that we might go through are both real and understandable. The term 'heartbreak' is not only a metaphor. When someone close to us dies or leaves us – someone like a romantic partner, a child, a sibling or a dear friend – the grief from that loss can put a strain on our heart; in some rare cases leading to death.[15] In most other cases, this separation or loss feels like a devastating ache. Because it is. A devastating ache.

The support of a caring loved one can, in many cases, soothe (but not take away) this kind of pain. When a loved one is kind, patient, supportive and understanding, and when we receive physical or emotional comfort from others, our body releases oxytocin which can, over time, help to soothe some of our pain. This doesn't mean that our pain will be gone. Like placing ointment on a severe burn, it means that we can over time learn to soothe ourselves. Like giving a hug to a bereaved person at

14 Higa, et al. (2002); Kemp, et al. (2012); Xu & Roberts, (2010).
15 Rostila, et al. (2013); Stroebe (2009).

a funeral, physical and emotional comfort isn't going to bring back the person who has died. But, sometimes, offering this kind of support can significantly help the person while they are grieving, while they are going through the worst day of their life.

Most people, at one point or another, experience an excruciating breakup, one that can rattle us, making us feel like our very essence was stolen from us, like things will never be okay again. This is what happened to Carrie (this is not her real name). Steve, Carrie's fiancé of two years, suddenly told her that he was no longer interested in her. He said that he didn't love her anymore and moved out of their shared apartment the very next day. He refused to process the breakup with her after he moved out, blocked Carrie's phone number, and blocked her on all social media.

When Carrie came in to see me in therapy, it had been over a year since she and Steve had broken up. Carrie said that she couldn't move on because she couldn't understand what had happened in their relationship. There were no signs that Steve wanted to break up, so she understandably felt blindsided and lost. She'd spent the previous year combing through their entire relationship wondering what she'd done wrong.

'It shouldn't be like this,' she kept saying, 'We should have been married by now. Every day, I see the reminders of the life that I should have had, the life that was stolen from me, in my reminders and on my calendars. My friends keep telling me to just move on. To forget about him and find someone new. But me, I just feel so lost. And abandoned. And alone. I keep thinking that if only I had done something different, we'd still be together.'

Carrie's pain is completely understandable. Not only did she go through an excruciating breakup, but in not allowing Carrie the chance to ask him questions and have closure, by blocking her on his phone and social media without her first processing their breakup, Steve robbed Carrie of the opportunity to find acceptance of the ending of their relationship. When a breakup or a loss of a meaningful connection happens suddenly, such as it does in some relationships, sudden deaths or in cases of ghosting, we are forced to pick up the pieces of our shattered hearts. We are left with a million questions; questions often related to our illusion of control: *What could I have done differently to prevent this from happening?* And left without definitive answers, we will often make up our own – usually with self-blaming narratives because they allow us to believe that so long as we learn from this devastating experience, we ought to be able to prevent this kind of pain from occurring in the future.

The truth is that whether the person that suddenly left our life was a family member or a dear friend, grief is what we are *supposed* to feel. Grief is a natural and necessary emotion for healing. Some people might encourage you to 'focus on the positive' or to 'just be grateful for what you have'. But this kind of *gratitude shaming* and *toxic positivity* is not only unhelpful, it can actually be harmful, as it can interfere with your natural grieving and healing process.

I view grief, any kind of grief, whether it is grieving someone who has died, or grieving the end of a relationship or friendship, or a lost opportunity, as equivalent to food poisoning – we need to *process* it in order to let it out of our body. This means that your instinct to grieve is the right one. If you want to lie down for a day or two, or seven, or twelve, to just cry, allow yourself to do that. But focus on feeling your pain, not on running away from it.

Your reactions to grief and loss are necessary and understandable. Your reactions to other people's behaviours, including their actions of racism, sexism, homophobia, transphobia, fat shaming, slut shaming, violence and infidelity, are not only allowed, they are also important and necessary. You are allowed to feel the way that you do for as long as you need to.

Give yourself the permission to take your time with your pain. There is no timeline on recovery from what you are going through. There is no 'one way' to cope with it. And it makes sense for you to have a hard time letting go of what happened to you.

Give yourself the permission to genuinely grieve over whatever loss you are going through, let yourself feel whatever feelings are arising in you and see if you can notice and name them, even for a brief moment. This is already a big step. This is already you regaining a part of yourself as opposed to running from what's happening inside your body.

So, this week if possible, see if you can observe what you are thinking and feeling about a specific situation that is causing you physical or emotional pain.

Ambiguous Losses

Situation	Thoughts	Feelings
For example: Carrie is devastated over her breakup with Steve	'I should have done something different to stop it from happening'	Sad, angry, guilty, frustrated, confused

It Shouldn't Be This Way

Chapter 3
Feeling Stuck

Every life-changing experience, be it the loss of a function, a job or a friendship, or the death of a loved one, can be excruciating. Acquiring a new illness, like cancer, migraines, organ failure, autoimmune disease, or having a stroke can forever change our life and our abilities. And what makes it even more challenging is that many other people might fail to understand how challenging our adjustment to 'normalcy' might be. Because there is no 'normal' in these experiences. How can there be? These experiences, they change you. Forever.

And how could they not? After all, that's exactly what they are supposed to do.

I am not here to give a silver lining to your experience. I am not here to tell you to be grateful for what you still have or to focus on the fact that 'at least it could have been worse'. To do so would be both to insult and to discount the mountainous grief and trauma that your experience has caused you.

What I am hoping to do, however, is help you to navigate your own mountain of pain, just as others helped me.

If you got a chance to notice your thoughts and feelings mentioned at the end of the previous chapter, what did you observe? Chances are, that you noticed that you might be on a path that you don't want to be on. You might feel like you so badly want to change the reality of what happened or what is currently happening but might feel stuck instead. You might be working in a job that you hate or be struggling to accept your trauma, or perhaps struggling with what is happening worldwide in terms of countless other people's suffering.

And it makes sense that you feel this way. Of course you would want to change things. You feel this way because you care. You care so much that it hurts, tearing at the very core of you. Going through any kind of a trauma, such as a loss of a friend or a family member, being betrayed or abused, or seeing a loved one suffering, can make us feel that the world is an unsafe place to live in. It can potentially make us wonder how we can possibly move on, how we can possibly live through this.

What many people fail to understand is that traumatic experiences, such as sexual assault, abandonment, or the death of a loved one might happen quickly but the impact that they have can last for years afterwards. For example, survivors of sexual assault often report that they feel as if their life is never the same after that event. And it is true – their life isn't the same after going through such a horrific experience. Similarly, people who have lost a family member due to an accident, such as when a loved one is killed by a drunk driver, report that one moment changed their entire life and they couldn't be more accurate in their assessment.

Every experience that we go through changes us. According to Newton's law of physics, for every action, there is an equal and opposite reaction. And that means that for a violent trauma, such as an assault, abuse or a tragedy, there will be an equally violent reaction in our body, one that might take years to settle, if at all. What it also means is that there might be an opposite reaction too, an empowering one, one that can show you just how resilient you are, even if in the moment you might not feel that way. Many people who go through something traumatic later experience panic attacks, depression, feeling 'sensitive', feeling easily overwhelmed or hopeless, crying at seemingly 'small' things, and being frequently overstimulated. These reactions are not a weakness. They are our body resettling after an internal earthquake, resettling in order to strengthen over time. Don't fight this process, allow it to take place. That shaky sensation that you might feel – that is your adrenalin running protective drills inside your body. When feeling over-stimulated or depressed, that's your body recognising that you need to step away and care for yourself in order to charge up and get back into the battle.

Several years ago, I was working with a client, let's call her Jessica. Jessica was in a terrible car accident fifteen years prior but that wasn't what brought her in to see me. After the car accident, she'd started having unusual symptoms, ones she never had before. She noticed that she was severely afraid of getting ill. She would wash all her vegetables, sometimes for 30–45 minutes, worried about the bacteria on the vegetables causing her to be fatally ill. She would scrub all counters that the raw vegetables had touched. If she then accidentally touched the counter where she'd previously put her vegetables, she would need to wash all her clothes and scrub her hands until she felt that she'd sufficiently cleaned them. Jessica was diagnosed with OCD at that point and couldn't understand why she'd developed it. In addition to struggling with OCD symptoms, she also had a very hard time accepting that she'd developed ODC in the first place. She believed her diagnosis, but kept saying, 'But I just don't understand why I developed this. I've never had this before.'

To make matters worse, Jessica's OCD caused a lot of problems in her marriage. Her husband was highly critical of her symptoms, frequently yelling at her, calling her 'crazy' and telling her that he was ashamed to be seen in public with her. Whenever they fought, Jessica's symptoms would worsen, causing her to spend a lot of time engaging in her compulsions, such as scrubbing and washing.

When her husband had an affair, he blamed it on Jessica, 'If you weren't crazy, I wouldn't have cheated on you.'

Jessica's husband never allowed her to bring up the affair nor was she allowed to ask any questions about it. She never had the opportunity to process what happened to her, in terms of the car accident, her sudden onset of OCD, and her husband's infidelity. And needless to say, after the infidelity, her symptoms worsened. By not being allowed to process her trauma of being in a car accident, as well as her new symptoms of OCD and the excruciating pain of the affair, Jessica didn't have a chance to face her emotional pain. And because of that, her symptoms intensified.

Our trauma, our grief and our pain can all feel like a self-perpetuating fire energy. This energy builds and builds and builds. And it needs somewhere to go. In Jessica not being allowed to discuss her trauma, in not being able to face and manage it, she suppressed it, trying to control it. As a result, it diverted into something she thought she could control, meaning that she tried to control how many times she washed her hands and the cleanliness of her kitchen surfaces. And the more she tried to control them, the longer and more intense her compulsions became.

In addition to the trauma of her car accident and her husband's infidelity, Jessica was also subjected to years of mental health stigmatisation and emotional abuse at the hands of her husband. He criticised her for her anxiety, for crying about her anxiety, for feeling down on herself, for her OCD and for her gaining weight as a result of her medication. It seemed that there was nothing that Jessica could do to please him. She tried hiding her symptoms. But it didn't work. She tried doing everything he asked of her. But it didn't work. He was still highly critical of her.

I remember in one of our sessions, she looked defeated, saying, 'There is nothing I can do to make him happy.'

I looked at her and nodded, 'You might be right.'

She looked back at me. We looked at each other for a while and then she said, 'It's true, isn't it? It didn't hit me until just now. There is absolutely nothing I can do to make him happy.'

Somehow, she seemed a little bit less defeated just then. 'I guess . . . I guess, he will just never be happy.'

'And you?' I asked her.

She thought about it for a while. 'I . . . I haven't been happy in years . . . I've spent so much time trying to make him happy, trying to prevent bad things from happening, that I'm not really living. But I think it's true. No matter what I do, he will not be happy. And maybe I won't be either. Not with him. Not like this.'

It took her over a year to leave. It wasn't easy. She doubted herself every step of the way. Yet somehow, accepting the fact that she couldn't make her husband happy allowed Jessica to see his flaws. It allowed her to see how unworkable their relationship was. And it gave her the strength to find her freedom, not only from her (now) ex-husband, but also from her OCD. She still has anxiety. She still has some obsessive thoughts. But they rarely interfere with her life now because, in her case, she's no longer trying to control something that isn't working for her.

No one should ever have to be bullied or shamed for who they are or for what they are going through. Sadly, like Jessica, many individuals have experienced emotional abuse, as well as bullying and shaming, for having a mental health disorder. Others might experience abuse or prejudice based on their sexual orientation, gender identity, race, religion, or other aspects. In other words, at the times when we might be in the greatest need of support and compassion, we might also face harsh criticism, abuse and judgement from others, sometimes from the people closest to us, the people whose opinions we might value the most. After a while, other people's harsh voices might become our own and we might shame ourselves, echoing the voices of our abusers.

When we shame ourselves, we might be recreating the stigma that we have faced. We might also find ourselves feeling incredibly alone in the darkness of our worst experiences. Internalised shaming, much like the illusion of control, creates a mind trap, making us believe that we *should not* feel the way that we do, that we *should not* need other people's support, and that we *should not* still be feeling stuck in the past.

Yet, again, how could we not? Anyone in the same situation would feel the same way.

Perhaps, then, the problem is not that we shouldn't *feel* this way. Perhaps the problem is that we were never previously *allowed* to feel this way. This pain. This grief. This anger. It is so big and so powerful. You might fear that if you allowed yourself to face it, it would break you.

But the truth is – this pain – it isn't coming. It is already here. And if it is here anyway, then maybe, just maybe, you might be able to face it.

It is completely okay if you are not ready yet. It makes sense. You've spent this entire time trying to keep this pain at bay, so of course you might not be ready to face it, perhaps not yet. I find that one of the most challenging aspects of opening up to our pain is the loneliness of our painful experiences. Healthcare magazines are referring to loneliness as 'the new smoking'[1] because of its numerous problematic effects on our health. And so, if everyone you know isn't helping you, or worse, criticising you while you are already drowning in the pain of your experiences, it makes sense that it doesn't seem like you can ever find the strength to face it. That is exactly why support groups or

1 Schimpff (2019).

therapy can be especially helpful in that regard. Finding someone, at least one person that you might be able to open up to and talk with, can help to alleviate the terrible burden you are carrying.

Some people erroneously believe that talking to other people about what they are going through is a sign of weakness. And in fact, many of us were raised to believe this fallacy. Yet, science tells us that we are meant to be social. It tells us that social support improves our mental health over time and the lack of it might worsen mental health outcomes.[2] This means that being able to share what you are going through with at least one understanding person can make a difference over time. It will not bring back what you might have lost. It will not take away what you are going through. But it can give you the support that you need to get through some of the biggest challenges of your life.

Many people might be apprehensive about seeing a therapist. Some people might have been taught that therapy is 'for crazy people' or that 'therapy is airing your dirty laundry'. Some people have family members who might harshly object to them going into therapy.

I would know. My mother was furious with me when I began therapy, stating that I should be able to figure things out on my own. I imagine that she was probably just afraid. Perhaps afraid of what my therapist might think of me, of her, of our family. She might have been afraid of other people in our family finding

2 Wang, et al. (2018).

out about my going to therapy and that somehow it might be a reflection on her. I can never be sure. But I know that it was a big obstacle for me.

Not all therapists will be the right match for you, just as not all jobs are a good fit. The first therapist I saw asked me why I'd come in to see her. When I told her that I was feeling depressed, she said, 'You're fourteen! What do you possibly have to be depressed about? You have parents who care about you. You have a home. You have food. What are you possibly sad about?'

I shook my head. 'I guess, nothing. I'm fine. Thank you,' I finally said, trying to conceal the sarcasm in my voice.

And with that, I left. Four minutes into our session.

The next time I saw a therapist, I was twenty-five years old. I decided to go in after the sudden death of my dear friend.

I had a lot of reservations about going. I was scared of having the same therapy experience, of being shamed about my feelings, and being misunderstood. However, my therapist was incredibly kind and professional. She helped me process my friend's death and my many emotions, among them, anger.

'I'm not angry!' I said to her the very first time she pointed out this emotion.

'Ah, my mistake,' she said. 'It's just . . . Every time you mention your parents . . . you seem . . . I don't know . . . you seem like you're feeling anger. But not just anger. Rage.'

I didn't know why tears ran down my face like a rainstorm the instant she mentioned the word 'rage'. I was so angry about her accusing me of being angry that I was furious with her for even saying it. She was kind and patient and understanding.

She didn't push me until I was ready to talk, which wasn't for several weeks.

'You know that thing you said about my parents? About me being angry?'

'Yes?'

'I ... I never realised ... I ... never thought ... I wasn't allowed to feel ... I never felt angry. Or I never knew that I did.'

It was the first time that I realised the extent of the oppression of my emotional expression by my family and culture. Anger was a forbidden emotion, especially for girls. As was depression. And pretty much all emotions with the exception of guilt and gratitude. If I wasn't grateful, then I had better be feeling guilty for not being grateful because 'others have it much worse'. This kind of toxic gratitude shaming exists all over the world and creates narratives that we aren't allowed to grieve, rage, or rebel. It turns us into servants of a broken system, punishing ourselves over time, eliminating any additional need for external punishment because we become the executioner of our own worth.

And we might be so stuck in these mind traps that we do not even realise that we are in them, caught like an Ouroboros, an infinite serpent that is depicted as forever eating itself. And if we are, in fact, blinded to our own experiences, there will be no way out. Once we realise that something feels wrong, that we are stuck, that we feel angry, frustrated and hungry for a change, that is when the real healing begins.

Chapter 4
The Way Out

As human beings, most of us are pre-wired for connection and a sense of belonging. And when those needs are not met, when we are rejected, neglected, or shamed for having basic human survival needs, such as a hug or reassurance, we might fail to develop healthy attachments with others, as well as with ourselves.[1] The need for social support and belonging is so essential to our survival and development that extreme cases of child neglect, in which children are deprived of physical and emotional comfort, can lead to detrimental neurological, physiological and psychological changes.[2] This means that if you were brought up in an environment with the constant threat of rejection or abandonment based on your behaviour, your appearance, your emotions, your ability or another aspect of you, this threat of abandonment could lead to you struggling to accept yourself, potentially perpetuating self-abuse, self-shaming and *internalised self-oppression*.

The heartbreaking truth is that in some circumstances we may have been shamed, abused and rejected right when we were in the greatest need for compassion and empathy. We may have already been struggling with self-acceptance, with

1 Scarlet (2020).
2 Chugani, et al. (2001).

feeling like *the other*, struggling to fit in. When others made fun of or rejected us for the very thing that we were already insecure about, that rejection may have become a kind of external oppression. We may have translated that rejection to mean, 'this part of me is unacceptable, and therefore, until I change it, I cannot be lovable or acceptable enough.'

One of my clients, 'Sarah', shared with me that her mother used to threaten her with abandonment. Whenever Sarah didn't finish her homework or didn't clean up her room, her mother would say, 'Look at yourself. You should be ashamed of yourself. How can I be a mother to someone like you? That's it! I'm going to leave you and be a mother to another girl, a better girl than you and you will be all alone, and nobody will love you.'

This is an example of emotional abuse and its wounds can affect someone forever. Being shamed can make a person believe that they aren't worthy of being loved. The threat of abandonment from a parent, a friend group or a significant other is also a form of abuse. The threat of abandonment, in which rejection is essentially used as a form of punishment, creates an unsafe environment. The person being abused through punishment by rejection might be led to believe that their relationship with the other person is not safe or stable and is at risk of ending. This means that the person being threatened with abandonment might be constantly holding their breath, waiting to be rejected, waiting to be punished, all the while feeling almost like a slow death is coming. When we are living under a constant threat, we are in survival mode and we are unable to fully function and grow.

And, eventually, our abuser's words may become our own. We might begin to shame and punish ourselves worse than anyone else possibly could. We might call ourselves names when we look in the mirror; we might shame ourselves for making a mistake or for struggling with depression or anxiety. In all of this, we are amplifying the abusive messages we received from our abuser – your feelings aren't allowed, who you are isn't allowed, what you want isn't allowed.

Yet, all of these are allowed and necessary. You are allowed to be you. You are allowed to do, be and identify the way that you do and the way that you are. You are allowed to feel how you feel. In fact, feelings are meant to be felt, that is why they are called *feelings*. And feeling them is not a surrender. It is an act of rebellion. It is an act of saying, 'I feel what I feel, and I am allowed to feel this way, damn it!'

One of my clients, 'Laura', reported that at one of her first office jobs, her company vice president (VP) told her that her hair was 'unprofessional'. She was the only Black woman in her office and the only one given a comment on her natural hair. She was told that her hair violated the office policy and that she needed to style it in order to look 'more professional'.

After receiving this feedback, Laura then spent hundreds of dollars getting her hair straightened. She reported she was angry at her VP but also found herself feeling self-conscious about her hair. She would spend a long time looking at herself in the mirror, trying to adjust and straighten her hair. She would silently compare herself to other women at the office, women whose hair was naturally straight, shaming herself for her own hairstyle.

'My hair became my sense of worth, on which I judged myself on any given day,' Laura reported. 'When I had a "good hair day", I felt good about myself. And when I had "a bad hair day", I felt like I was in a class below everyone else, just wanting to hide and stay quiet. My hair became the definition of me, instead of my work, and what I actually had to offer.'

It wasn't until Laura quit that job and started law school that she learned that this kind of practice of requiring employees to change the appearance of their natural hair is a form of discrimination. And despite that, it wasn't until 2019 that California became the first state in the United States to officially ban discrimination against people's natural hair types or hairstyles. Other states were and are still slow to follow.

To this day, people are judged by the colour of their skin, their hairstyle, their dress style, their body type, as well as by the way they cope with mental and physical health issues, and the way they respond to the events in their lives. People who grieve over a miscarriage are often told that they aren't allowed to grieve in the same way as people who have lost an older child. People are judged and rejected over their sexual orientation or gender identity, being told that they 'bring shame to their family' or that they need to 'choose' not to be who they are.

For so many of us, we might start believing these lies that somehow we are not enough; that our pain, our story and our feelings don't matter; and as a result, we will not be able to accept the reality that this pain that we feel is not only allowed, but is necessary. By acknowledging the pain inside you, whether it is your physical pain or the pain of your emotional wounds, or (as it is often the case) the excruciating combination of the two, you can stand up against societal oppression of your experiences. Over time, by acknowledging and getting to know the pain inside you, you can find your own voice and make space for this pain. Because the only way out is through.

A few years ago, I was working with a client, 'Olivia'. Olivia's father and sister were killed in a horrific car accident. In one day, she lost two people that she loved, while also taking care of her ailing mother. Olivia came into my office two weeks after their deaths. She had not been sleeping, she was having chest pains and non-stop shaking throughout her body. Her doctor sent her to see a cardiologist, and after multiple tests the doctors told Olivia that her symptoms were likely caused by stress and anxiety.

Olivia is a very powerful woman. She is a college professor; she is also a successful business owner and the head of her household. When I told her that she was having panic attacks as a reaction to her grief, she said, 'I get it, doc, but I don't have time to be having panic attacks right now. I just buried two members of my family, I have a mom, a husband and two daughters to take care of. I have classes to teach, a business to run and my charities to support. What can I do to make this go away?'

We sat for a moment and then I said, 'Olivia, what does being able to help your family and to do your work mean to you?'

She said, 'Everything. It's my life, doc. I gotta get back in there.'

I nodded. 'And that is exactly why we need to go slow. We

need to go slow in order to allow you to go fast, like you always do.'

'I don't understand,' she said.

'This experience changed you. How could it not? And that means that we start here. Exactly where you are right now. Not where you were before this accident. But right now. Today.'

She breathed through the tears. 'You don't understand. I feel like I'm stuck . . . wandering around a dark forest and I just don't even see the light anymore. How do I get out?'

I leaned toward her and nodded, 'The only way out is through.'

She took a breath, nodding in understanding.

There was a pause between us.

Then she sat back, allowing her shoulders to release and fall. And then she sobbed.

Many people might fear that if they allow themselves to face the pain inside them, that it would break them, tearing them to pieces. However, most people find that the opposite is true. The more we run from this pain, the bigger and more painful it becomes. When we face it, when we walk through it, as if walking through a dark forest, eventually we begin to see the light. And wisdom. And eventually it becomes easier to breathe and find ourselves again, or maybe find ourselves for the very first time.

This process – facing your inner and outer struggles – it's kind of like your very own Phoenix moment. A Phoenix is a magical creature found in many fantasy books. At different points of its life, the Phoenix bursts into flames. It burns and falls into ashes. And then, the Phoenix rises again, stronger than ever before.

And when we are facing our pain, a part of us dies in that moment. And it makes sense – you aren't the same person. Not anymore. The reason why you can't 'just get over it' is because you aren't meant to; that isn't how it works. You are meant to channel it and use it to discover the very core of you. It's painful and of course, it burns. Because you are a goddamn Phoenix and you are on fire!

Chapter 5
Avoidance

When you live life to the fullest, you are inevitably going to experience pain and suffering. It does not mean you are doing something wrong. What it means is that you are doing something right. When you care about something, you are likely to experience a full spectrum of emotions, from the tear-jerking kind of joy to the heart-wrenching kind of pain. That is what living is all about. Allowing yourself to have the full spectrum of emotions is a response to what life might bring so that you can better navigate the way you go about things and move closer to what you care about and be able to stand up for what you believe in.

Any attempts to avoid dealing with our grief or trauma are likely to exacerbate our suffering, further extending our pain.[1] When you break your arm, you care for it, you wrap it, and you give it time to heal. We need to do the same with our hearts. When we feel broken, we need to wrap ourselves in a hug or a warm blanket. When our body feels broken, we need to give it time to heal.

Healing starts with an acknowledgement that something has been taken from you. It could be your health, your loved

1 Betz & Thorngren (2006).

one, an opportunity, compassion or respect. And so, of course, you might feel devastated, numb and angry, often at the same time. When others say things like, 'Why can't you just let it go?' or 'Why can't you just be normal?' or 'You are causing yourself to feel this way', it can make your blood boil. As it should. Because those statements are examples of oppression, in which you are led to believe that your feelings and reactions aren't allowed. And after a while, we, too, may begin to oppress ourselves with harsh criticism.

Avoidance of acceptance is a form of internalised self-oppression, which tends to backfire – it worsens our symptoms in the long term.[2] Our emotions are kind of like pressure in a fizzy drink. When we get shaken up, the pressure builds, and that pressure has to go somewhere. Have you ever shaken the fizzy drink bottle before opening it? What happens when you open the bottle after it's been shaken? I imagine that you might have experienced the mild (or sometimes, the intense) explosion that can happen when a fizzy drink bottle has been shaken enough times.

Why do you think it happens that way? The pressure inside builds and builds and builds. All that pressure needs somewhere to go. If you don't release it, if you keep bottling up and suppressing that pressure, it will eventually explode. Just like you.

But what happens if you slowly open the bottle over time? Releasing a little pressure over time can help the fizzy drink to

2 Thompson & Waltz (2010).

settle, so that it can return to its usual state, or even become flat (without the pressure build-up) over time. In a similar way, we may be able to slowly open up to some of the emotions and pains that we have been suppressing and release some of the built-up pressure.

Some people might say, 'But I've been building up this pressure for so long, I'm afraid that if I open up to it, I will not be able to face it.' And that's a valid point. The longer we have been running away from feeling or processing something painful, the more painful it will be when it inevitably surfaces. And here is what we know about emotions: just like fizzy bottle drinks, they don't explode forever. When faced with a trigger of our past, we might be hit with a heightened amount of grief, loss or anger. It might feel like an internal explosion. We might sob. We will grieve. And like a fizzy drink bottle, our emotions will also settle down over time. This experience is painful, yes, but it is also necessary.

The purpose of this book is to help you learn how to slowly open up that bottle of pain, so that it can ease some of the excruciating experiences you are already carrying, as well as learn how to cope if that built-up pressure erupts unexpectedly.

First, let's talk about how that pressure builds up internally. Let us imagine that someone at school or in your workplace is bullying you. They might make fun of you, call you names, or exclude you from important projects or activities. This will understandably make you sad and angry. Listening to mis-judged guidance from other people, you might keep avoiding these feelings, but they will accumulate, making you furious, depressed or, as it is the case for some people, suicidal. For many, feeling suicidal isn't about not wanting to live, it is about wanting to escape the reality of their pain and suffering. It is about wanting the pain to stop. Given how much pain and suffering so many people who have suicidal thoughts endure, it makes sense. This amount of pain would be too much for anyone.

So, how do we safely navigate this amount of suffering?

The first step is to acknowledge that suffering exists, to allow ourselves to notice that we are in pain (physical, emotional, or both) and to acknowledge that it is happening right now in this moment. This. Right now. This is a moment of pain and suffering. And you are allowed to feel this way.

In fact, the more we avoid this pain, the more we suffer.

Avoidance is a lot like addiction or gambling. In the short term, it might feel 'better' not to think about the pain of what you are going through. And it makes sense that when something bad first happens, you might need a few minutes, hours or days to step away from it in order to fully process it.

However, in the long term, avoidance becomes addictive. We grow dependent on it and start to rely on this unhealthy coping mechanism more and more in order to try to feel 'better'. We might hide out in the 'safety zone' of our comfort behaviours, like sleeping or bingeing on our favourite TV shows, our favourite foods, or our favourite video games. For the record, there is nothing wrong with watching TV shows, having tasty food, or playing video games. But when we engage in these behaviours *purely to avoid feeling bad*, we inadvertently create a trap for ourselves. So long as we engage in these avoidance behaviours, we might feel well enough, or avoid feeling as bad as we fear we might. This avoidance comes with a price. The moment you stop engaging in avoidance behaviours, you might have a rebound of the pain you have been avoiding. This is exactly what happens with alcohol and other substances. When they are used to keep the pain away, that pain returns with a vengeance the moment that the given substance leaves your body, creating a greater and greater need for more avoidance behaviours and often exacerbating the suffering that we are already going through.

The more we avoid feeling pain, the more we end up feeling it in the future. The more we try to suppress our pain, the more excruciating it feels and the more it persists. And, because emotions are an 'all-or-nothing' package deal, when we try to suppress heartbreak, we also suppress joy and connection.[3] The more we numb, the more disconnected and alone we might feel. This resulting numbness can feel both painless and also excruciating at the same time.

It is in those moments that some people start to think about suicide. Suicidal thoughts are natural responses to trying to escape pain. Our mind naturally tries to find all possible solutions to reduce our pain. It might feel lonely and unbearable at the moment and it may seem like the pain will never end.

The pain might not end but it is likely to change over time. The only way out is to reduce avoidance of our feelings and experiences because our painful emotions aren't the perpetrators of

3 Brown (2015).

abuse. They are the result of it. And paradoxically, the more we try to run away from what we are feeling, the more we run into those same emotions and sensations.

For many people, their avoidance behaviours may include hiding out in their room or their flat. Initially, hiding out in your safety zone might help to reduce your feelings of anxiety, depression or grief, but in the long term, avoidance of venturing outside that safety zone will likely exacerbate these feelings. If you see your home as your safety zone, then you might imagine that the moment you step outside of that, you will not be able to manage your emotional or physical pain. When we believe this idea, it makes sense that we would want to hide away in our safety zone for as long as possible. However, the more time you spend in your safety zone, the smaller your safety zone becomes over time, and the larger your unprocessed emotions grow. This means that the more you avoid the outside world, the more you are actually rooming with the very emotions you were trying to avoid.

A few years ago, I was working with a young man, let's call him 'John'. John struggled with social anxiety. He desperately wanted to be liked and accepted but was also terrified of being judged or rejected. Many of us fear being socially rejected. How could we not? We survive by making meaningful social connections, so of course we want to be liked and accepted. That makes sense. However, avoiding all social interactions in order to reduce the risk of being rejected doesn't make sense because it can create the very outcome we fear the most – that we would be rejected or no longer invited to social events. For years, John would avoid going to social gatherings, even when his college classmates would invite him out. He feared being rejected and would hide in his room. The more he hid, the fewer invitations he received over time. His worst fear came true not because he put himself out there, but precisely because he did not. We think that by hiding out we are keeping ourselves safe, but what we are ultimately doing is slowly churning out the script of our biggest nightmare.

Common avoidance behaviours can include (tick off all that apply to you):

- Cancelling plans
- Procrastinating on doing your work
- Trying to control and predict every aspect that you can
- Perfectionism
- Blaming yourself
- Blaming others
- Drinking, smoking or eating purely to manage how you feel
- Restricting eating
- Over-cleaning
- Shutting down
- Distracting yourself to avoid your feelings or memories
- Forcing yourself not to think or feel something
- Avoiding telling someone how you feel
- Playing video games or watching TV shows purely to avoid feeling something uncomfortable or to avoid doing something uncomfortable

- Yelling at people or being defensive
- Oversleeping
- Overworking or overcommitting yourself
- People pleasing
- Endless scrolling through social media

After a while, our ability to tolerate uncomfortable experiences becomes non-existent and even the smallest discomfort puts our system into overdrive.

Why does that happen?

By constantly running away from an uncomfortable situation, you are subconsciously telling yourself, *I can't handle it*. After a while of thinking like this, your body believes you. So, whenever you are experiencing an emotion that you normally try to avoid, your body will likely react as if you are in danger by releasing fight-or-flight-or-freeze chemicals and elevating your heart rate and blood pressure. When that happens, if you then step away from the situation, you are reinforcing the belief that you are unable to handle that emotion, meaning that in the future, your body is even more likely to react as if you are in danger when you feel that same emotion again. In addition, by utilising your avoidance behaviours, you are also not giving yourself the opportunity to figure out which situations are actually tolerable and which ones are not.

However, the opposite is true, too: by learning to trust ourselves to spend time with our painful internal experiences, we might diminish the struggle with these very experiences. After all, these painful feelings, thoughts and sensations aren't your enemy. They are a part of you. They are a part of the pain that you have been through, a part of your origin story. By learning your own origin story, you might be able to understand the function of these painful internal experiences, as well as how to navigate through them.

Chapter 6
Origin Story

Every hero's journey begins with a struggle. Every hero, real and fictional, faces tremendous suffering as a part of their call to action. For some, their origin story includes the loss of a loved one. For others, it has to do with being hurt or persecuted. And still for others, it might have to do with facing a tremendous injustice. Your origin story understandably changed you. It would change anyone. It might have changed you, but it doesn't define you.

My own origin story began in Ukraine, where I was born and raised. When I was not quite three years old, there was a massive explosion at the Chernobyl Nuclear Power Plant and my family and I, along with most people who lived in Ukraine and the neighbouring countries, suffered from acute radiation poisoning. To this day, I am still waiting for my Spidey Senses, the Invisible Girl's powers of invisibility and force field control, or Hulk's super strength, and never did I end up becoming a giant Ninja Turtle. However, my reality included spending most of my childhood in and out of hospitals because my immune system was severely suppressed and couldn't fight even a simple cold. Because of that radiation exposure, whenever the weather changes, I experience severe migraines, which sometimes lead to seizures.

Growing up in a Jewish family, I witnessed first-hand what anti-Semitism can look like when the levels of violence and discrimination against Jewish people made it dangerous for us to remain in Ukraine. When I was twelve years old, my family and I were able to immigrate to the United States as refugees. And like a lot of twelve-year-olds, I was severely bullied in school. Kids would ask me if I was 'radioactive', 'contagious', or if I 'glow in the dark'.

To say that being bullied was painful would be an enormous understatement. The regular teasing, public humiliation and social ostracism was excruciating. And the physical and emotional abuse I was going through at home made it unsafe for me to exist anywhere. That entire year I just wanted to die. It wasn't just because of the bullying, the abuse or my health problems. It was because at that age, whenever I tried telling someone how depressed or anxious I felt, I would either be made fun of in school or punished at home.

Most people I tried interacting with at that age would say that I needed to 'just focus on the positive' and 'change my attitude'. I was told, 'what do you have to be sad about? You have parents who love you and you live in America. You have food, you have a home and a cat. You are being ungrateful. Look at those other people who have nothing. Just be grateful and focus on the positive.'

The problem was that during that entire year, there was nothing positive for me to focus on. Even brief moments of pleasure, such as the taste of a chocolate ice cream, would be overshadowed by the bruises, the bloody noses and the panic attacks related to being terrified of being hurt or publicly shamed. Because I was repeatedly told that my emotions and 'negative perceptions' weren't allowed, I silently shamed myself for feeling bad. I would say the kinds of things to myself that were even worse than what others would tell me, such as, 'What is wrong with you? Suck it up! Stop feeling sorry for yourself, you idiot! No wonder everyone hates you. You should just die because you are nothing. Nobody cares about you and nobody will ever love you.'

After a while, I became a mere shadow of myself. I relied on being a good student and a helpful person. I focused on people-pleasing to run away from how awful I felt about myself. I tried to act and say things that would create the most peaceful environment possible. Anything to avoid a fight or a conflict. I laughed at jokes that made me cringe. I sided with people who were rude to me, and I allowed others to mistreat me because I was convinced that my own emotions were wrong. I thought that I wasn't allowed to feel sad or angry. Or, for that matter, that I wasn't allowed to be or feel altogether. My focus turned to helping others not necessarily because I wanted to, but because I was desperately trying to survive. I would often come to school at least an hour early to help my Earth Science teacher set up her classroom. I would stay after school or spend my lunch period tutoring other students or helping teachers grade tests or homework assignments. I would say 'yes' to anyone who needed me at any time, while ignoring my own needs and forgetting that I was a person, too.

Then, when I was sixteen years old, everything changed

when I saw the first *X-Men* film. The X-Men are a group of mutants, each of which has a genetic mutation, which allows them to have certain abilities. All of the X-Men had been bullied and all had experienced prejudice. Most had been oppressed, shamed and excluded for being different.

I felt like I was watching my life on the screen. I watched, hardly breathing, as the X-Men came together at a school in which they not only learned to strengthen their abilities, they learned how to support one another. They learned the importance of care and belonging and how loving connection can heal some of the most painful wounds.

The character that immediately grabbed my attention was Storm, who had the ability to control the weather. My entire life, I had felt controlled by the weather and seeing Storm on the screen put me in awe. Seeing her using her powers made me rethink my own connection with the weather. I realised right then that my origin story did not make me a victim. It made me a survivor.

Seeing the amount of suffering that the characters went through when they experienced oppression and bullying, seeing the pain and the loneliness in their faces made me realise that I wasn't alone in feeling that way. And more importantly, it made me realise that not only were my internal experiences allowed, they were necessary for me to understand and process what I had been through.

As I looked around the completely sold-out cinema, there was not a single dry eye that I could see; I realised that every single person in that audience knew exactly what the characters had been through. Maybe not everyone had been exposed to torture and radiation like Wolverine, and maybe not everyone had lost their parents in the Holocaust like Magneto, but everyone in that audience could understand what it meant to feel *different* and how important it was to feel a sense of connection and belonging.

Somehow seeing the fictional characters' experiences of loneliness, bullying and oppression, allowed me to better understand my own. More than that, it gave permission for my unprocessed painful emotions to arise. Feelings of grief, depression, anger and longing all rose inside me, all at the same time. Something about the process of *allowing* these emotions to be there, welcoming them, feeling them alongside the X-Men on the screen and the hundreds of moviegoers in the audience, took the shame and stigma out of this experience. I cried during most of the film – tears of grief and sorrow that I had been repressing for over a decade. And also, tears of connection, joy and gratitude that I could share this moving experience with other people, both the audience members and also the characters on the screen.

As I left the cinema that night, I reflected on why that film had had such a profound effect on me. I realised that most of us become prisoners not only of our own origin stories, but also to the erroneous messages we receive from others about how we *should* feel about what we have been through. The common societal message (and a major misconception) is that expressing and feeling painful emotions, such as sadness or anxiety, constitutes a form of weakness. And yet, if expressing our emotions, if facing our internal pain and opening up to our internal suffering is one of the most terrifying experiences that we might face, then does it not also mean that it is the most courageous act of which we are capable? It isn't the avoidance of internal darkness that makes one brave, it is the willingness to face it. Because suffering itself is not a weakness – it is the foundation upon which we can find our inner strength.

What if everything you have been through and everything you are feeling is a part of your origin story? And an origin story is just that – the beginning. It is the beginning of your heroic quest, your jumping-off point. But the rest is up to you.

If you are willing, perhaps we can take a few moments to examine your own origin story. Many people go through numerous losses, excruciating physical or emotional pain and feelings of loneliness and alienation. Just like our favourite superheroes, or real-life heroes, we too have an origin story. An origin story can be a memory of a terrible tragedy, an accident or a moment when we decided to make different choices.

Take a few moments to consider your own origin story. Do you remember a defining moment that shaped you? Maybe an assault, abuse, rejection or the sudden death of someone you cared about?

Or perhaps it was numerous moments, trying times and experiences, which at the time felt unbearable, such as years of bullying, abuse or discrimination?

What would constitute your own origin story? If you are willing, please write down one or two sentences about your own origin story. You don't have to go into detail if you don't want to. Feel free to share as much or as little as you feel comfortable doing.

_____

_____

_____

_____

_____

_____

Now take a few moments to identify a personal hero. This is someone you see as a figure of ultimate wisdom and compassion. This could be a real person, such as a grandparent, a teacher, a mentor, a star athlete you admire, a creator or a historical figure you look up to. Or, it can be a fictional character, such as Batman or Wonder Woman.

If you cannot think of a personal hero, that is perfectly okay. See if you can think of a kind of hero you would like to have or look up to. What kind of qualities would your hero have?

_____

_____

_____

_____

Now, take a few moments to imagine that you have some alone time with your hero. Your hero knows exactly what you have been through, what your origin story is, and how it has shaped you. Your hero is understanding, supportive and encouraging. Your hero knows exactly what to say to you and what you may need to hear.

What would your hero say to you?

_____

_____

_____

_____

_____

If it is too difficult to think of what your hero may say, no problem. It happens to a lot of people. Take a breath. You can always try this exercise at another time.

None of the paths you have in front of you are easy. Perhaps none are definite or guaranteed. However, the one thing that we know is that you are meant to be here. You are meant to make a difference in this world. Your origin story does not define you. It is the mere beginning of your heroic journey. The rest is up to you.

Chapter 7
Acceptance vs Enabling

When some people hear the word *acceptance*, they might assume that it means being okay with what happened to them or letting people 'off the hook'. In fact, there is a difference between acceptance and 'feeling good' about what happened. In reality, acceptance refers to allowing yourself to feel whatever emotions naturally come up in response to what you are going through. It means acknowledging that the painful event(s) did take place, even though in an ideal world they wouldn't have happened that way.

For example, it might mean acknowledging that a loved one did, in fact, die, or that a person whom you trusted did, in fact, let you down. It doesn't mean you are happy about what happened nor does it mean being okay with the way you were treated. Rather, acceptance refers to giving yourself the permission to grieve and process these events in the way that makes sense to you. It means giving yourself permission to take as much time as you need to, regardless of how others tell you to feel and act. It means taking the time to process what happened to you. It means allowing yourself to experience any feelings that come up in response to this situation, including anger, grief, frustration or anxiety.

There is also a big difference between acceptance and letting people get away with doing bad things without facing any consequences. For example, when 'Ana'[1] came to see me for complex post-traumatic stress disorder (PTSD), she revealed that for many years in her childhood, her father sexually assaulted her. The abuse finally stopped when Ana was twelve years old. At twenty-two, Ana was finally able to report her father and press charges. Her mother, her siblings and her aunts and uncles were furious. They believed Ana that the abuse happened, but they criticised and shamed her for reporting her father to the authorities. 'How could you do this to him? He's your family! You need to accept it, forgive him, and move on. How could you be so selfish?'

When Ana and I started working together, she was confused. On the one hand, she wanted to hold her father accountable for sexually assaulting her for over ten years, all of which took place while she was a minor. On the other hand, her family's messages rang in her mind. She asked me if she should just 'accept it' and move on.

As I looked at her, someone whose eyes were filled with tears, someone who was robbed of her childhood, someone whose family members failed to protect her, my heart hurt for her. We talked for several sessions about the difference between *acceptance* and *enabling*. Specifically, we talked about the fact that *acceptance* in this case would refer to acknowledging that she was a survivor of childhood sexual abuse. It would also mean recognising that her family members failed to support her

1 Ana is not her real name.

when she was finally able to disclose her abuse history to them. Lastly, we talked about *acceptance* also referring to giving herself the permission to feel any emotion that arose in response to her abuse and her family's reactions in regard to her father's predatory behaviours. Ana was able to acknowledge that she felt 'angry, sad and disgusted', all of which were completely necessary and completely understandable emotional reactions given what happened to her.

We then talked about *enabling*. Enabling may look like compassion or forgiveness on the surface but it tends to be toxic and unhelpful to all parties involved. For example, when survivors of abuse are shamed into 'accepting and forgiving', they often experience re-traumatisation and further internalised oppression, which can lead to depression, PTSD, panic attacks, substance use or suicidal thoughts. This kind of 'acceptance' is not acceptance at all. It is *enabling*. Enabling refers to allowing unhealthy or abusive behaviours to continue. For example, true acceptance of a family member who struggles with addiction would mean holding their hand or visiting them in the hospital or at a rehab while they are going through withdrawal. On the other hand, giving them alcohol or other substances is neither an act of compassion nor is it acceptance. This kind of a behaviour enables the addiction to continue and the individual who struggles with addiction might never learn that they are capable of overcoming it.

In one of our sessions, Ana informed me that her family asked her why she was 'digging up' her past and airing the 'family business' like dirty laundry with her therapist. Sadly, many survivors of abuse receive the same messages – that the past should stay hidden and that survivors aren't allowed to stand up for themselves because of the way it might impact their families. Worse, many are blamed for upsetting others with their trauma stories. In those instances, the messages that the trauma survivors are receiving are that their feelings aren't important and that it is their job to make everyone else feel good and comfortable. As a result, the trauma survivor might be left alone with their pain while the perpetrator is able to continue their unhealthy behaviours without any consequences. And this is precisely what enabling looks like.

In Ana's case, her family focused on enabling her father rather than on trying to protect Ana's wellbeing. Oftentimes, we might unintentionally act to enable others when they are being overly aggressive, loud, pushy, or when they use 'guilt trips'. When people act in one of those ways, we might be more likely to retreat, give in and do what we can to appease the other person.

Some of us, like Ana, may have been taught that we need to 'stay quiet' and 'not make any noise' in order to prevent things from getting much, much worse. In the moment, it might feel as if we are being kind or accommodating when we give in or allow the other person to do or have what they want. In fact, we might often be praised for being accommodating and shamed when standing up for ourselves. And yet, no one benefits from you staying quiet, from you making yourself small, or from you downplaying your needs and feelings.

When I was sixteen years old, I worked as a receptionist at

an office. My boss, let's call him Scotty, was an older man, in his forties. Sometimes we would be alone in the office on weekends. Scotty would ask me to lock up the front office for a meeting with him. He would give me a stellar review of my receptionist skills and then ask me for a hug. As I would hesitantly approach him, he would do inappropriate things to me, as I would beg him to stop.

After three months, I finally got the courage to quit. I remember thinking that maybe I should say something to someone. I wondered if I should report him. But I never did. At the time, I didn't want 'to be difficult'. I thought that if I reported him, I would just be hurting him, his family and his business when it was easier to just 'accept' that it had happened and leave without making any trouble. It didn't occur to me at the time that what I was actually doing was enabling him.

To this day, I wonder if he ever did it to someone else. I realised more than a decade and a half later that by not reporting him I didn't just 'let him off the hook', I potentially put another young girl in the same predicament without him ever facing the consequences for his actions. A few years ago, I was able to call the office I worked in and verify that there was no ongoing abuse of any employee at that time. However, knowing that my inaction might have put another person in harm's way in the interim is one of the biggest regrets of my life.

What this regret has taught me is to stand up for what I believe in even if it makes other people uncomfortable. It taught me that acceptance means the recognition of what happened to you. Allowing yourself to acknowledge what you have been through and how you are feeling can be one of the most empowering steps we can take toward our own healing. Owning our truth, even if it makes other people uncomfortable, is what acceptance can look like.

Acknowledging what happened to us and what we are going through can allow us to empower ourselves, no longer hiding in the shadows of our past, but instead finding the drive in the anger and the injustice of it. The truth is that your life is a blank piece of paper and only you decide the kind of epic adventure that you might choose to embark on. You don't have to follow anyone else's narrative about how you should feel or act. You are your own person and you are the hero of your own journey. And so, perhaps, acceptance is the biggest act of rebellion that you can do. Perhaps it is the boldest way that you can stand up against the oppression that you have faced so that you can live your own life.

Rather than fitting into someone else's story about who you are supposed to be and how you are supposed to feel, maybe, just maybe, you are exactly who you are meant to be and maybe your most painful feelings are exactly how you are supposed to feel. Maybe behind the curtain of pain, trauma and tragedy is the door to your greatest strength. It does not imply that this process is easy or that it is supposed to feel *good*. Instead, it implies that perhaps allowing yourself to feel however you feel in the moment might allow you to power up over time to find your own path on which you are the hero of your own journey.

Chapter 8
Resistance and Fire

Several years ago, I had a minor disagreement with my partner. We were both frustrated with one another but were in the process of talking through our disagreement. I then wanted to give my partner a hug, but he refused, saying that he was still frustrated and didn't want a hug at that moment. Logically, I knew that he, just like any other person, deserved to set his boundaries and that he had the right to decide when he felt comfortable with physical affection. However, on an emotional level, I felt like my body was on fire. My stomach felt like it was being punched and twisted all at the same time. Everything somehow felt heavy but empty, too. I broke down, sobbing, which I don't often do. I felt like I was dying, and I wanted to die. For me, this isn't a common reaction and I was genuinely surprised at how much such a small action had affected me. I cried for over an hour and even my partner's subsequent hugs didn't make me feel better. I couldn't understand what was happening, except that I felt like I was drowning, and I could not stop feeling that way.

I didn't learn about emotional flashbacks until four years later. You might be familiar with the concept of a flashback in terms of remembering something bad that might have happened to you, like a car accident, a specific instance of abuse, or learning about a terrible tragedy. When we recall a specific event in this way, this is a *cognitive flashback.* On the other hand, an *emotional flashback* is one where we might not be actively remembering the traumatic event that we experienced but our body acts and feels as if it is happening right now.[1]

When we are having such a strong reaction, rarely does that reaction actually relate to the present situation. Usually, it deals with an old pain, one that has not only not healed but one that hasn't been allowed to heal. In my case, my partner not wanting a hug from me at that moment ripped open the door to my past, in which my mother used withdrawal of affection as an intentional punishment. When I was a child, if I did something that my mother found upsetting, such as not finishing my dinner or staying up past my bedtime, she would tell me that she was going to leave me.

She would say, 'You should be ashamed of yourself. I am going to leave you and be a mommy to another girl, one who listens to me. You will be all alone and nobody will ever love you.'

In some instances, my mother would start to put on her shoes or her coat to pretend to be walking out on me. As I would wail and beg her not to go, she would agree to stay, refusing to hug me, saying that I didn't deserve it. She would sometimes stop speaking to me, ignoring me for several days at a time and refusing to hug or reassure me that she wouldn't leave or that she still loved me.

Like many children whose parents used the withdrawal of affection as punishment, I learned to believe that if I wasn't

1 Walker (2013).

'a good girl' then I would be rejected and alone. As a result, I started people-pleasing in order to prevent people from being angry with me. This type of people-pleasing behaviour as a way of preserving our emotional safety is called the *fawn response*.[2] The fawn response is one of the most commonly utilised trauma responses in survivors of child abuse.

It took me several decades to realise that I was using the fawn response in order to foster secure attachments and to reduce the likelihood of being abandoned. This meant that for over thirty years of my life, I put other people's needs above my own, sacrificing my wellbeing to fit in and make others happy, even if it meant sacrificing my own mental and physical health. And years later, when my partner stated that he didn't want to hug me in that specific moment during our disagreement, the excruciating pain that I felt in my body was not at all related to him setting a very understandable boundary. Instead, that tornado inside my body was the primal scream of the little girl who was not allowed to feel, a girl who was threatened with abandonment and being deprived of love. It was the primal scream of someone who was breaking, someone who was suffering, and someone who was on fire.

I didn't realise it then but along with the decades of repressed pain was also a tremendous amount of anger, anger that I believed I wasn't allowed to feel or express. In fact, many of us are taught that we aren't allowed to feel angry, sad or anxious. That feeling these emotions is somehow a weakness.

2 Walker (2013).

Women, especially, are taught that feeling angry is unacceptable and de-feminising, while being taught that feeling sad or anxious makes them 'crazy', 'dramatic' or 'overly emotional'. At the same time, men are often taught that feeling sad is somehow emasculating and that anxiety is a 'sign of weakness'. Gender-fluid and non-binary individuals face even more oppression in terms of what they are told they are allowed to feel, as many are mistakenly told that gender identity is a choice. Hence, people of all sexes and all gender identities have been taught that emotions are something to get rid of, as if we are some kind of an alien android. Yet, even science-fiction droids are often depicted in an endearing light when they display emotions. In fact, one of the most prominent androids of *Star Trek*, Data, is on a constant quest to discover and understand emotions in order to become more human.[3] So then, why is it that as human beings we are praised for rejecting that which ultimately makes us human instead of being praised for humanity?

A part of being human means noticing and exploring every part of what makes us human, and that means recognising, feeling and processing our emotions. All our emotions are important and necessary. Each presents a vital piece of information that can help us to recognise what our needs are in the present moment. The more we may resist one particular emotion, the more it grows like a wildfire, eventually exploding during a seemingly small event, like what transpired between my partner and myself.

3 Scarlet (2016).

The truth is that there are no 'good' or 'bad' emotions. Your emotions aren't your enemies. They are all functional and informative, and if we listen, they can let us know exactly what we need. Here are a few examples of some of the emotions that we might experience and their potential functions. The more you observe your own emotions, the more you might be able to learn about your own needs, as well as how to listen to what your emotions are trying to tell you.

Emotion	Function	Example
Anger	To protect ourselves or others and take a protective or caring action	When someone is being mistreated
Depression	To let us know that we need to stop, rest and heal, reminding us to seek support or to support ourselves	Feeling depressed when we feel lonely, rejected or heartbroken
Disgust	To avoid toxic foods or people	Learning about someone's immoral actions
Embarrassment/ Shame	To avoid being rejected, to belong, to establish connection with others	When you make a mistake in front of someone

Empathy	To feel **with** someone else, to help and better understand others	When you feel sad learning about someone else's grief
Frustration	To preserve or expel energy when things are not going the way you would like	When someone repeatedly ignores you
Guilt	To learn which actions might not be helpful in the future	When you feel bad about saying something unkind in an argument
Happiness/Joy	To give our lives meaning, to remind us of what we care about the most	When your heart warms at watching people you care about being happy or when someone truly notices you and your efforts
Hate	Comes from pain, functions to try to protect us from further pain	When someone hurts us or hurts someone we care about
Hopefulness	To motivate and inspire change, to give us something to look forward to	Feeling hopeful about a new treatment strategy

Hopelessness	To alert us that something is not working, and we need to try some-thing new	When we realise that avoidance will not take away our emotional or physical pain
Irritability	To signal us that we might need a break or support	Snapping at someone even though they didn't do anything wrong
Jealousy/Envy	To look for reassur-ance and to seek emotional safety	When we compare ourselves to others, wanting to be assured that we are good enough
Overwhelmed	To signal us that we need support or guidance	When we have too many things to do and don't have enough resources (time, energy or money) to complete them all
Panic/Anxiety	To alert us that we need to rest, or seek emotional safety or reassurance, as well as a reminder to slow down and process what we are going through	When we have too many things to do and not enough time to do them; when we think that we are not good enough, or when we have not processed past grief or trauma

| Surprise | To alert us to new information, to keep us out of danger | When we saw some-one we did not expect to see |
| Vulnerability | To connect with others, to build emo-tional closeness and safety | Opening up to ourselves and others about how we feel |

As you can see, each emotion has a very important function, only a few examples of which are listed in this table. In order to learn more about your emotions, do not fight them. Get to know them. Listen to them. See if you can be curious about them and learn from them. Do not resist them – do the opposite – feel them, channel them, allow them. Use them.

The more that you have been avoiding these crucial parts of you, the more challenging it might be to study them. And that is okay. You don't have to rip open the grave in which all your emotions and all the past parts of you have been buried. Not all at once. It is okay to take your time. It is okay to start slow and get to know your emotions and the different unexplored parts of you over time.

When it comes to exploring painful memories or emotions, psychologists Kristin Neff and Chris Germer talk about the practice of *opening and closing*.[4] In this practice, you can allow yourself to open just a little bit at a time, exploring how you

4 Neff & Germer (2018).

feel. You can also close at any time if you are feeling too triggered and overwhelmed. As you start to feel safe enough, you can slowly and gently open up to your emotions and memories over time, and you can also close and step away from this practice at any time you need to. You never have to force yourself to feel any emotions or memories that you are experiencing. Everything you feel makes sense and you are allowed to feel any and all of it in your own time. You are the expert of you. You are the hero of your own story and only you get to decide what is right for you.

Take a breath.

Are you ready?

Chapter 9
What It Brings Up

At first, I felt dizzy. The world swam before my eyes like in some kind of a cartoon. *What's happening to me?*

I was ten years old and had just learned that my grandfather, my favourite person in the entire universe, had passed away. Just like that. Yesterday, we joked and laughed over the telephone, making plans to read and play together. Today, he was gone. *Dead.*

That word didn't make sense to me. It did in its logical form, but not in the actual gravity of it. It felt too big and too impossible to actually be true. The ten-year-old me couldn't understand how it could have happened.

When my father first told me that my grandpa had died, I said nothing. I just stood there as he gave me an awkward, one-armed hug. I don't think I hugged him back. I just stood still. Stoic. Numb. Confused.

Two hours later, I felt dizzy. And then, I couldn't breathe. My body began to shake and vibrate. I was sure that I was having a heart attack and would soon die, too, just like my grandfather did.

'What is the matter with you?' my older brother asked.

'I don't know . . . I just . . . I can't stop shaking.'

'Well, stop it!'

I couldn't.

'I'm going to die! I think I'm gonna die!' I started crying.

My brother slapped me across the face the way we see actors do in movies – usually a man slapping the 'hysterical' woman to get her to stop panicking.

Unlike the movies, the slap didn't calm me down. I kept shaking.

'Calm down, I said!' my brother roared at me.

I tried. I really, *really* tried.

I tried holding my breath.

I tried to silently yell at my body to calm down.

I tried stiffening my body on purpose.

But nothing seemed to work. The more I tried to fight it, the more vigorously I shook.

Then my brother went to grab a thick winter blanket, despite it being a hot summer day. He wrapped the blanket around me and held me. It was like someone popped a balloon with a long thin needle, because the moment I felt the warmth of the blanket and the comfort of his embrace, I sobbed. And soothed. Somehow the gentle kindness of this action was far more effective than him yelling at me to calm down.

I didn't know then that I was having my first ever panic attack. I also didn't know that trying to fight a panic attack (or any other internal sensation) is like pushing a colossal boulder up a slippery mountain. And what goes up, must come down – for every action, there is an equal and opposite reaction.

This kind of balance is necessary to keep us alive. Think about it. When someone drinks excessively, their body gets used to taking in alcohol. The alcohol affects the body in various ways. Specifically, it can increase the production of certain chemicals, such as dopamine and GABA, and decrease the production of glutamate.

Let's break this down. The first chemical we mentioned is *dopamine*. Dopamine is one of the 'feel good' chemicals and it is why certain substances that increase the amount of this substance in the body, such as alcohol, cigarettes, chocolate and other sweets or caffeine can become so addictive. We might crave them and wish to recreate that same 'feel good' sensation again and again.

The second mentioned chemical is *GABA*. GABA (gamma-aminobutyric acid) is an inhibitory chemical, which means that it can reduce some of the processes in your body, oftentimes making you feel more relaxed and less anxious. Since alcohol increases this chemical in our body, it is one of the reasons why some people feel more comfortable talking to other people after they consume a few drinks.

Finally, *glutamate* is an excitatory chemical, responsible for our paying attention, concentration, memories (both pleasant and unpleasant memories) and in some instances, anxiety. Since alcohol reduces the production of glutamate in our body and increases the production of GABA, it can create a kind of a double anti-anxiety effect, allowing some people to take a short break from their painful feelings and memories.[1]

1 For more information, see article by Bowirrat & Oscar–Berman (2005).

In order to keep us well-balanced, our body will then create an opposite effect. Hence, when the effects of alcohol have worn off, our body will underproduce dopamine and GABA, and also overproduce glutamate. All of this is done to ensure that our body does not go into some kind of a shock or a seizure, and otherwise stays in homeostasis. If we kept consuming alcohol and our body also did not adjust its chemical production, continuing to produce the same amounts of GABA and glutamate, we would likely become very ill. Since we are putting a foreign substance (i.e., alcohol) into our body, a substance that produces those chemicals, our body tries to compensate by adjusting the production of these neurotransmitters in order to try to keep us healthy.

This is why after the effects of the substance have worn off, we are likely to feel more depressed (because of lowered amounts of dopamine in our body) and more triggered and anxious (because of lowered amounts of GABA and heightened amounts of glutamate in our body). This is also why, over time, people are likely to consume more and more of a specific substance (such as alcohol) in order to try to get the same kind of a temporary 'feel good' effect or an escape from the pain of our past. Additionally, when people first attempt to quit a specific substance, they feel awful for a few days – their body has been so used to overproducing some chemicals and underproducing others, that it will take a few days for it to catch up. This explains why suddenly stopping the use of certain substances, like alcohol, can sometimes lead to seizures within the first few days and should be done with medical consultation. After a little while of not using the substance, most people are able to readjust and start to feel better on their own without relying on using said substance.

Avoidance in general is kind of like substance addiction. Whether we use substances or continuously avoid talking to others about how we feel, these only two things can make us feel better in the short term but can create problems in the long term. Avoidance behaviours can feel like an addiction in that we might depend on them more and more frequently over time. In many cases, we might find ourselves becoming oppressed by our own avoidance behaviours in a way similar to (or worse than) how we were previously oppressed by others.

The more we avoid our feelings and memories, the more our body will try to create a sense of equilibrium once again by bringing the past to our attention. This will eventually lead to a kind of an internal explosion that is large enough for us to pay attention to – a panic attack, a migraine, feeling sick to our stomach or having a breakdown. Some people develop obsessive or compulsive symptoms when trying to control their grief or trauma. In some cases, OCD can manifest in people having intrusive thoughts of harming themselves or others, or committing inappropriate or violent acts – something an individual would never actually do. This is yet another example of how when we try to control our emotional pain by suppressing it, it can come out in other ways (in this case, through intrusive but harmless thoughts and images that many people have).

Given how much you have already been through, of course it makes sense that you might wish to run away from your pain.

After all, it might bring up past shame, grief or trauma, as well as the countless toxic and oppressive messages that we were taught about how our thoughts, feelings, behaviours or needs were supposedly not allowed or unacceptable. And of course, after a while, facing those emotions, thoughts and memories would understandably feel like 'too much'. It is not only the painful event itself that we are reminded of when we face our internal pain, it is also the superimposed message that some-how we are not allowed to feel this way or that this situation was somehow our fault.

For example, one of my clients, 'Vicki', was fat-shamed her entire life. Her mother and her two older brothers would con-stantly tell her that she needed to lose weight. Her mother would sign Vicki up for countless gym classes and send her to fat camps when Vicki was growing up. Her brothers teased her and made fun of her. Her brothers inherited their mom's slim build and no matter how much they ate or what type of food they consumed, they never gained weight. Vicki, on the other hand, was shamed about all her food choices, and was made to feel that her weight made her unattractive. Vicki's mom would often say, 'You need to lose weight if you ever hope to get married.'

Vicki was the first person in her family to complete her master's degree and to become an educator. And yet, no matter how much she accomplished, she stated that the only thing she ever thought about in terms of her self-worth was her weight. She would shame herself for her looks, often comparing her-self to others. She would walk into a store or into a classroom and immediately take a look to see how many thin people there were versus how many people who looked like her.

She stated on several occasions, 'I feel like people who are thinner than me are in a different class than me. Like I'm not worthy. Like I'm second class, you know?'

If Vicki ever allowed herself to eat a candy bar or a slice of pizza, she felt the need to hide it from her family and her partner. She would often hide food in her room and when she felt particularly bad about herself, she would eat more than she wanted and then would report feeling sick. She stated that she was so ashamed of even *wanting* to eat something that her family would consider unhealthy, that she would eat in secret and would try to use food to escape her feelings.

In our therapy together, Vicki and I worked on changing her relationship with her food and with herself. We worked on Vicki allowing herself to have the food that she wanted to eat when she wanted it. In one of our sessions, I asked Vicki to bring in a candy bar of her choice. She practised giving herself the permission to have the candy bar because she wanted it and eating it for the pleasure of eating it, rather than to run away from her emotions. Specifically, we practised mindful eating, where Vicki was allowed to have as many candy bars as she wanted while truly enjoying them and reminding herself that she was allowed to enjoy food as her siblings did.

When Vicki started to consume food in this way, her eating began to change. She ate what she wanted when she wanted it. She ate to nurture and support herself instead of eating to run away from a painful emotion. She started speaking up against fat phobia, first supporting other people on social media, and eventually, standing up for herself and setting a boundary with her family members, 'I am a person. My body might be different from yours and that's okay. I am allowed to eat what I like to eat just as you are. You wouldn't judge a thin person for eating a kind of food they like, so please don't judge me.'

When we reduce our avoidance behaviours, it opens the door to us facing the pain we had been running from all those years. In some situations, we might remember the pain we had long forgotten or realise that certain situations we have lived through were more painful than we initially realised. Essentially, avoidance can be a defence mechanism against our internalised shame. That shame is nothing more than our childlike innocent way of trying to belong. We might punish ourselves for merely being human, all the while not realising that who we are is not only acceptable but also lovable. Utterly and completely lovable. What you do, who you are, how you feel, and what you have been through – these do not only make you lovable, they are some of the most lovable things about you.

For most of us, when we first open up to the pain of our past, there might be eruptions of emotions, oftentimes sobbing. This is a good thing. This is your body healing. And recharging. And eventually, the tears settle, and we are left in a more stable, more peaceful place in which we don't have to run from our past anymore.

Sometimes acceptance practice can bring up the pain of the past abuse, abandonment, shame, rejection or heartbreak.

What It Brings Up

Too often we might have been met with shame and criticism when we needed someone to comfort and reassure us. And over time, that critical message becomes our own self-critic, an internal defence mechanism against further abuse.

For many of us, we might form an automatic assumption that if we judge ourselves first, we might be keeping ourselves safe from further judgement and abuse by others. Many of us berate ourselves for our appearance, performance, setbacks, abilities or struggles. The kind of profanity and otherwise foul statements that we might use for ourselves, many of us wouldn't use even with our biggest adversary. And it seems that in times of our greatest distress, many of us are likely to be even harder on ourselves than usual.

One reason for us being more likely to use self-criticism during times of high distress is because we might believe that we aren't yet ready to face the pain behind the wall of this self-bullying attack. Because behind that wall is a history of abuse, grief or rejection. For many, there might be a generational or intergenerational trauma of experiencing racism, misogyny, homophobia, fat phobia, bullying, ability discrimination and other forms of abuse or violence. There might be the kind of trauma that brings us to our knees when we think of it. And that is exactly why some people are more prone to self-criticism than self-kindness.

Sometimes, when we experience kindness from others, we might suddenly become overwhelmed with grief. When we receive love and kindness from others, it can bring up the memories of the past situations in which we needed kindness but didn't receive it.[2] For example, when a kind friend validates you or says something kind when you are angry, it might remind you of all the times you were previously shamed for feeling this way. It is usually when we are feeling safe enough, cared for enough, and emotionally well enough that we start remembering more of our past. If you are starting to remember more instances of your past pain, it likely means that you are healing. This process is gradual and slow. Take your time, feel free to open and close to this pain whenever you need to. Remember that you are a warrior, facing a fire-breathing dragon.

You see, some people get up and go to work. Other people have to fight a slew of dragons just to get out of bed. And so, if you are battling five dragons with one hand, and trying to write your report with the other, then it makes perfect sense that your report might not be as pristine and timely as it otherwise would have been, had you not been fighting off all those dragons. If you are having a hard time concentrating on your work or other responsibilities because you are fighting the dragons of your past, it makes sense. Give yourself the permission to take your time to heal. This is especially true when you believe that you have no time to slow down. That's right – the less time you seem to have for you, the more time you actually need to take for yourself.

Take a breath. Take a moment. Count your dragons. How many dragons did you already face today? How many just to

2 Neff & Germer (2018).

get out of bed? How many to get to this point of the day? That's already impressive!

And speaking of getting out of bed, if you struggle to get out of bed when you wake up, you aren't alone. It turns out that there is a reason for the fact that getting out of bed can be challenging when we first wake up, especially when we are already struggling. You might have heard about *cortisol,* a stress hormone that is involved in our stress response, alongside another stress hormone, *adrenaline.* The amounts of cortisol can be measured through blood and saliva tests and the graph overleaf demonstrates the typical cortisol levels seen in people who are going through stress, as well as people with relatively little stress.

What do you see? You may notice that the levels of cortisol tend to be highest in the morning time, right around the time that most of us would be getting out of bed. And since cortisol is a stress hormone, it means that getting out of bed in the morning is one of the most stressful things you do each day.

So, if you have already gotten out of bed today, congratulations! You already did the most stressful thing of the day. You have already faced one of today's biggest dragons, and that means you can do anything.

If you have not yet been able to get out of bed today, if you need a little more time, if you need a few more minutes, hours or days to be able to get out of bed, that is okay, too. You are not being weak. You are being wise. You are being a warrior, protecting the little child within you, letting them heal in the way that maybe that child wasn't allowed to heal before. This, right

Diurnal Cortisol – Chronic Stress

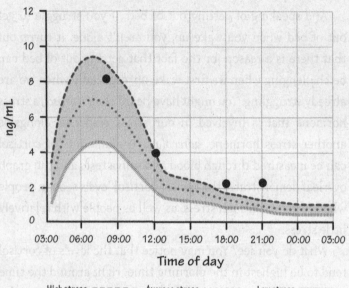

High stress ▬ ▬ ▬ ▬   Average stress • • • • • •   Low stress ▨▨▨▨▨▨

now, this is you healing, recharging your own battery, healing your own wounds, so that when you are ready, you will not only face your own dragons, you will also help other people to face theirs.

This is a painful process. Rather than walking around with the poison of your past inside of you, give yourself the time to process it and let it out of your body. Accepting that this pain is here and allowing yourself to face it, this is you being the rebel that you are. Remember that you don't have to face all your pain at once. You can open to and close off from your pain as you need to, slowly and gradually. This is how you heal, so by all means take all the time that you need.

Chapter 10
No Regrets

I love Halloween. I love the carved pumpkins and the pumpkin spice lattes. I love dressing up and decorating the house with flickering lanterns, smoky cauldrons and toy bats. And one of my favourite parts of Halloween has always been sharing the joy of it with my friends.

During my last year of living in New York, I decided to throw the ultimate Halloween party, one my friends and I would remember forever. I invited my friends and approximately twenty of my fellow graduate students. I prepared all kinds of spooky treats and turned the house into a kind of a haunted mansion. There were light-activated screeching bats, sound-sensitive screamers and creepy hands moving around the candy bowl. I also bought a few pounds of dry ice to put into the big plastic cauldrons, which I placed all around the house to create a smoky effect.

Unfortunately, as my guests started to arrive, one of them informed me that one of the plastic cauldrons had started to leak. I discovered, to my horror, that most of the cauldrons had holes at the bottom and the water from the dry ice was leaking out onto the floor. I grabbed a mop and started cleaning it up.

My partner suggested that we take out the dry ice and forget about having the smoky cauldrons, but I couldn't let it go. *After all,* I thought, *it was such a great mood setter.* I simply could not allow myself to have a Halloween party without the dry ice effect, and so I spent the entire party mopping the floors. All six hours of it.

My friends told me that it was the best Halloween party they had ever been to. But I missed it all because I was unwilling to accept that we could have a party without the smoky cauldrons. I put so much pressure on myself to make the party 'perfect' that I forgot to attend it.

When we run away from imperfection, we also run away from ourselves. Life is meant to be messy and trying to clean it up causes us to miss it altogether. Trying to hide behind the oppressive messages of how we *should* be and how we *should* feel can lead to us missing what matters most to us.

'The more you fail to experience your life fully, the more you will fear death,' says psychiatrist Dr Irvin Yalom.[1] And in fact, the more we focus on perfectionism, to-do lists, people-pleasing and running away from who we are, the more we might fear death and the more regrets we might have at the end of our lives.

Australian palliative nurse Bronnie Ware spent her career working with people who were nearing the end of their lives. In spending a lot of time with people on their deathbeds, she realised that most people had a number of regrets about how they had spent their lives. She was able to record her observations and found that most people's regrets fall into one or more of the following five categories:[2]

1 Yalom (2008).
2 Ware (2012).

No Regrets

1. I wish I'd had the courage to live a life true to myself, not the life others expected of me.
2. I wish I hadn't worked so hard.
3. I wish I'd had the courage to express my true feelings.
4. I wish I had stayed in touch with my friends.
5. I wish that I had let myself be happier.

Does this mean that we are all doomed to be filled with regrets at the end of ours? No, of course not. Having the awareness of the most common regrets can actually allow us to take our lives in a different direction.

Why is it that it is so hard for so many of us to be true to ourselves and to spend our time in a meaningful way? Many of us might have an easier time focusing on our productivity than on spending time with people that matter to us. Many of us attribute our self-worth to our productivity, as well as to our achievements and our appearance. However, at the end of our lives, those things cease to matter. At the end of their lives, most people don't say, 'I wish I spent more time on my to-do list.' Instead, most wish they had more time to spend with people who matter most to them.

Perhaps hiding behind productivity and achievement can allow some of us to avoid facing the universal truth that we are all imperfect. Perhaps, focusing on perfecting ourselves can allow us to temporarily escape the pain of our past and the anxiety about the uncertainty of our future. And yet, none of these allow us to fully live in the present, to fully be *here* in the moment, no matter how overwhelming or uncomfortable this moment might be. And this unwillingness to face the emotions of the present moment comes at a heavy cost: the cost of not living your life.

Here are just some of the costs that our avoidance behaviours might present:

- Missing out on time with our family
- Missing our friends
- Not taking chances and missing opportunities
- Pretending to be someone you're not
- Constant 'What if I'd only tried' regrets

Each time you make a choice to avoid something either by focusing on perfectionism, by using a particular substance, by cancelling your plans or by procrastinating on something meaningful to you, ask yourself what are the costs of this behaviour? What am I giving up by engaging in this behaviour and is this how I want to spend my life?

When we tell ourselves that we cannot have friends over until our house is spotless or that we cannot take a dance class until we lose weight, or that we cannot start dating until we no longer feel anxious, what we are really doing is procrastinating – putting off living. And before too long, life might pass us by and we might regret not having spent more time with people who have passed away, the people we thought we would have had more time to see. We might regret focusing so much on trying to live up to some unrealistic standard; we might have missed out on living our lives because we were too busy living in accordance with other people's notions of our worth.

Conversely, the willingness to say, *F**k it, it's important to me, and I am going to do it even if it doesn't feel good in the moment!* can allow us to start living now, no longer fearing death because we have lived a life full of meaning.

And so, if you weren't avoiding all the people, places and situations that you do, if you took the chance to be true to yourself, accepting the fact that it might not feel good in the moment, what would your life look like then?

PART II:

Acceptance in Practice: The How

Chapter 11
Gentle Acceptance Practices

Acceptance is easier said than done. This practice isn't at all like turning on a light-switch. With a light-switch, it is either on or it is off. Acceptance practice is quite different from that in that it can fluctuate many times throughout the day while ranging across a wide spectrum. One moment you might find yourself completely willing to explore the emotions that arise when you remember your past trauma, and a few hours later, you might be too overwhelmed to think about it. At other times, you might find yourself somewhat willing to explore your emotions, at least in small amounts of time.

However you experience acceptance today is perfectly okay. This is not an acceptance boot camp. There is neither an acceptance drill sergeant nor an acceptance competition. It is perfectly okay for you to take each experience slowly and to observe your own needs. This means that you don't have to force yourself to suffer. Instead, this process can be gentle and kind. For example, you can utilise the previously mentioned 'opening and closing'[1] techniques. As a brief reminder, you can allow yourself to be open to noticing whatever thoughts, feelings and behaviours arise and it is also okay for you to take a

1 Neff & Germer (2018).

step back from this practice by closing and taking a break from these experiences.

I like to think of this practice as adjusting the shower temperature. If the water is too cold, we can adjust it in little bits at a time, gradually turning the knob to make it warmer. But you don't have to blast hot water all at once for the risk of scalding yourself. Just like gradually making your shower water warmer and warmer until it reaches a more tolerable temperature, you don't have to burn yourself with your painful emotions. You can open up to them slowly, one at a time, allowing yourself to 'cool off' and to step away whenever you need to.

It can also be helpful to consider rating your emotional experiences as a kind of 'temperature level' from one to ten. For example, if you are so overwhelmed by an excruciating flashback or pain that you are having suicidal thoughts or are otherwise in the state of an emergency, we would call this 'a ten' on the temperature level system. If your current emotions, thoughts and sensations present as a moderately tolerable experience, we can consider them 'a five' on the temperature level system. It can be helpful to think about what your current temperature level is and what you can tolerate, when you need to step back, and when you are able to try again.

Everyone has a different system, please honour yourself to find yours. For example, I know that for me, I can function when I am at levels one to seven. When I am at levels eight to nine, I need to step away from my responsibilities, cut down on my work, and reach out for support. If I am at level ten, everything else must stop, and I need to focus 100 per cent of my energy on healing, soothing and supporting myself. And unless your life is in danger (e.g., if you are in a violent relationship or in a war zone), you don't have to force yourself to do more than is absolutely necessary for you to survive when you are at level ten.

By noticing our 'temperature' levels, we can be more mindful of the way that different emotions and flashbacks show up in our body. If you struggle with anxiety, panic, depression, trauma or addiction cravings, you might notice that your body goes through certain physiological changes when you have these experiences. For example, you might notice that when you are feeling anxious, your shoulders become more tense, your jaw clenches, your chest tightens, or your stomach feels queasy. Perhaps your heart pounds faster or your breathing becomes more shallow.

None of these symptoms are dangerous. In fact, these are the same physiological sensations that we also experience in moments of joy, such as when we are dancing or laughing. The main difference between having these physiological reactions in moments of joy and moments of anxiety is that we are more willing to accept these sensations in one situation than the other.

In order to make your intense emotional experiences more tolerable, we can break up these experiences into separate components. For example, if you are having a panic attack, you might notice the following physiological symptoms:

- Racing heart
- Shallow breath

103

- Tension in your shoulders
- Tightness in your chest
- Stomach discomfort
- Dizziness
- Tightness in your jaw
- Feeling sweaty
- Tingly hands or feet
- Racing thoughts

Once you can notice and name all of the uncomfortable sensations you are experiencing, you can practise acceptance by focusing on one of these at a time. You might start with the sensation of the racing heart. If physically possible, I invite you to place one hand or both hands on your heart centre to make full contact with this part of your body. And then, focusing on just this sensation – the racing heart – allow yourself to sit and breathe. It might be uncomfortable but it isn't dangerous. Take a few breaths and see if you can sit while just focusing on *allowing* this one sensation for approximately two minutes.

After you have completed this exercise, move on to another sensation, like the discomfort in your stomach. If physically possible, place one or both hands on your stomach to make full contact with this sensation. Allow yourself to breathe and allow this sensation to be there. See if you can fully focus on this sensation for two minutes while breathing. Then, switch to another sensation.

This practice can also be applied to physical pain and nausea. For pain and nausea, see if you can spend at least two minutes with each sensation, allowing yourself to feel it while breathing. As someone who has chronic pain, this practice is very familiar to me. Whenever my pain would spike, I used to tense my shoulders, clench my jaw and hold my breath, gasping from the excruciating pain that I was going through. This tensing, breath-holding and clenching are all common reactions to physical or emotional pain. And they are also all resistance behaviours, which inevitably spike pain even higher.

We naturally tense and hold our breath when we are anxious, angry or in pain, and yet these actions actually make us feel worse. As counterintuitive as it may seem, focusing on unclenching and breathing in those difficult moments can allow us to get through them. Lowering our shoulders, focusing on breathing out rather than holding our breath, and loosening up our jaw may not make our pain go away, but it might make the *experience* of our pain more manageable. Hence, the purpose of these exercises is not necessarily to make the symptoms go away but to help us better tolerate these sensations.

When dealing with racing thoughts, it might be helpful to write them out or to speak them out loud and record them with a voice recorder app. After you have written out your thoughts or recorded them, read them over out loud or listen to them on the app. What do you notice about the experience of having these thoughts inside your head versus listening to them being read out loud? By externalising your thoughts in this way, you might be able to reduce some of the pull that these thoughts have on you. Inside our own mind, these thoughts feel big, scary and overwhelming. When we write them out, these thoughts may have less of a hold on us. Another externalising practice includes saying the thought out loud over and over and over again until its words lose meaning.[2]

The main point of this exercise is to *allow* your thoughts to be there, to create a stream of release rather than trying to suppress these thoughts or bottle them up. Additionally, if the same thought keeps showing up for you, it is perfectly okay to write about it over and over again. It is also perfectly okay to keep thinking and talking about the same event over and over again. When we have been through something painful or traumatic, we may need to process that event many times over in order to make sense of it. And yes, it means that all those people who told you that you have been talking about a particular event 'too much' and that you need to 'just get over it by now' were wrong. It may mean that you need more time to process what you are feeling and thinking. Allowing yourself to write about it and process it, even if just with yourself, can potentially allow you to accept how you are feeling over time. Acceptance here doesn't mean that what happened to you was okay. Rather, it means making room for how you are feeling about it. And with this kind of an acceptance, there can be healing.

There is no one way to practise acceptance. As you practise, you might find your own way that works for you. One way you can begin your acceptance practice is through the *Valve Exercise* below:

2 For more exercises like these, check out a great book by Dr Steve Hayes, called *Get Out of Your Mind and Into Your Life*.

Valve Exercise[3]

Have you ever seen an air mattress or bicycle tyre or a beach ball? Each of these has a little valve which allows it to be inflated or deflated. In a similar way, we can practise letting some of the pressure or tension out of our body.

Take a few moments to notice any areas in your body where you might feel tense, such as in your shoulders, your jaw, your chest, your stomach, your forehead or the top of your head.

Imagine that each of these areas has a little valve that you can open to allow some of the pressure out. If possible, see if you can actually pretend to open a valve in these parts of your body, one at a time. Each time you open a valve to let some of the pressure out, see if you can sit back and breathe for a few moments, allowing your body to settle as you are practising this exercise.

What did you notice?

Practising this exercise can allow you to release some of the built-up energy in your body, which can ease your internal tension. This, in turn, can potentially make it easier for you to practise acceptance of your internal sensations altogether.

Another exercise that focuses on the acceptance of our internal sensations is called *Letting the Dog off the Leash:*

---

3 This exercise initially appeared in Scarlet, J. (2021) *Superhero Therapy for Anxiety and Trauma.*

Letting the Dog off the Leash[4]

Imagine for a few moments that you are taking your dog to a dog park (even if you don't actually own a dog). When the dog is on the leash, he is probably excited, hyper and cannot wait to be let off the leash. But once you take the leash off, the dog can run around freely to let some of his energy out until he feels calm and settled.

Now, we are going to do a similar exercise with each of these sensations. We are going to start with the least uncomfortable, the least distressing sensation from the ones you recognised on pages 103 to 104. Got one?

Okay, now imagine that you can zoom in your attention to only focus on this symptom or sensation. For example, if you picked 'sweating' then focus your entire attention now on just noticing how sweaty you are feeling in this moment.

Great! Now, we are going to imagine that you take this sensation to the dog park and take the leash off. That means that just for a few minutes, we are going to only focus on this sensation while allowing it to be here, allowing it to be as strong or as weak as it needs to be.

If you are willing, I am going to ask you to close your eyes and focus only on this one sensation and fully allow it to be here, as if allowing it to run around in the dog park.

Ready?

Go!

---

4 This exercise initially appeared in Scarlet, J. (2021) *Superhero Therapy for Anxiety and Trauma*.

How did it go? What did you notice? Was it tolerable just to focus on this sensation?

Would you be willing to try another one?

See if you can focus on each of these sensations one at a time for at least 1–2 minutes.

What did you notice over time?

The more we can let our emotions 'off the leash', one element at a time, the easier it can be for us to face and experience these emotions over time. In my case, I spent sixteen years holding onto the pain of what Paul's actions of faking his own death had put me through. I couldn't accept that someone could treat me this way. And it was, in fact, unacceptable behaviour. I also couldn't accept the way that I felt whenever I thought about it. I felt so angry that I couldn't even bring myself to examine how hurt I also felt. Other people's messages made it worse. Whenever I would bring it up with someone, they would tell me that I needed to stop thinking about him. Because I wasn't allowed to talk about him, I also didn't allow myself to think about how I felt about what had happened between us.

Then, nearly fifteen years later, I learned about acceptance practices. I recognised that my inability to process my pain from this event was holding me back from living my life. I decided to make a commitment to practising acceptance skills regularly. Whenever I thought about Paul, I would write about how I felt, allowing myself to grieve over the way I was treated. I allowed myself to feel angry, sad, frustrated or any other emotion that came up for me. I would make an appointment with my feelings and allow myself to feel them. It took a year. And one year after

I started this practice, something shifted. I acknowledged that what he did was not okay, that his behaviour was still unacceptable but that I could accept that it had happened. I wasn't happy about what had happened between us but somehow I was no longer angry about it.

It was then that I found out that Paul's younger brother had died. I reached out to Paul to offer my condolences, and the next time I was in New York, we met up for lunch. It was strange seeing him in person. Strange because I was able to see him as a human being for the first time; not as a monster that hurt me, but as a person who did something bad who was also someone going through grief. He apologised for his actions and something in me was laid to rest.

I realise that I was very fortunate to be able to receive closure, something not all of us can get. In cases of child sexual abuse, sexual assault, intimate partner violence and other similar situations, meeting with the abuser might not be safe. Such violent actions are never acceptable and stay with us forever so we can allow ourselves to feel however we feel about them. It is okay to feel angry; it is okay to be sad; it is okay to grieve even years after the terrible event has happened to you.

Many people might still feel sad over the loss of their relationship even if their partner was abusive toward them. Many of us might have conflicting emotions toward certain people, ranging between feeling hurt by them and missing them. All of these emotions are understandable, and you are allowed to feel them all.

Of course, your past pain might still be affecting you today.

This pain, what you are going through, it keeps hurting for a reason. It keeps reminding you that your voice still needs to be heard, that you are allowed to be angry, sad and devastated. It is reminding you that YOU have not gotten a chance to speak yet, to REALLY tell YOUR story, to really process it, to really feel. So, please take your time with it. Schedule an appointment with your feelings. Schedule some time every day just to cry, to vent, to feel, to speak, to write, to allow yourself to be and feel however you actually feel.

This is your call to freedom. And you have waited long enough to be heard. You deserve to be heard. Your voice matters. Your pain matters. Your feelings matter. You are allowed to feel however you feel for however long it takes you. And that is where you might find the root of your innermost strength.

Chapter 12
The Core of the Onion

Opening up to the trauma of your past can bring up a lot of memories that you might not have previously processed, thought of or even remembered. I refer to this process as *peeling the onion*. Each time you allow yourself to feel a painful emotion and sit with a painful memory, you peel a layer of your trauma. The more avoidance there has been in the past, the more layers there might be in your trauma onion.

In the past, it may not have been safe for you to peel these layers back. You might have been in survival mode. You may have been in an abusive setting; you may have been barely hanging on without a supportive person by your side as you were facing some of the biggest challenges of your life. And so, it made sense that you had to put the processing of these events on hold. In fact, it was probably wise.

When people experience the biggest horrors of their lives, such as seeing a loved one killed in front of them, being abused by a family member, or going through a natural disaster, they focus on survival. In that moment, trauma-processing and acceptance of one's grief isn't only impossible, it would possibly be unsafe. It could prevent that individual from being able to focus on getting out of that situation alive.

Most of us focus on survival first, and it is only when we

have reached safety (physical or emotional safety) that the dust starts to settle and we may begin to experience depression, anxiety or the excruciating effects of grief. Sometimes the emotional pain is so bad that we may fall into a deep depression. Sometimes, when we have too much unprocessed pain, it will turn into panic attacks as a way of releasing the deep underlying emotions that you may have suppressed. Sometimes the pain might get so bad that you may think about suicide.

If you ever feel that way, please know, you are not being 'dramatic' – you are burning from the excruciating pain of your past. Burning like the Phoenix that you are. It hurts in this moment because it is supposed to. Because of everything you have been through. And it does get better. It really does. It hurts right now, and it might seem like the pain will last forever. And then, if you hang on just a little longer, the pain passes. And it becomes easier to breathe.

That sensation when your emotional pain is excruciating, when it feels like there is no hope, when you feel raw and naked in your pain – that is the core of the onion. The core of the onion is the place in which you have the biggest contact with your feelings and so, naturally, it is also the place in which you experience the greatest amount of emotional pain.

For me, as I started to open up to the pain of my ex-partner faking his own death, I also remembered something else. I remembered being assaulted by my boss when I was sixteen years old. I remembered a history of a past assault by an ex-partner who forced me to drink when I was a minor and then took advantage of me. I remembered severe physical abuse by two of my family members.

These past traumas poured out of me and I felt like I was suffocating. But then, over time, I felt like I could breathe again. Over time, the pain begins to subside, and things fall into place again.

When you are at the core of the onion, everything else has to stop. It may seem too overwhelming to face it, yet avoiding it altogether will not be helpful either; in fact, it is likely to make you feel worse in the long term.[1] Just like food poisoning, your past trauma needs to be processed in order to leave your body, so that it isn't continuously poisoning you from the inside.

Here are the seven steps for getting through the core of the onion:

1. **Name it.** Just naming the experience can allow you to know what's going on, so that you can properly support yourself. For many of us, being able to name what we are going through can make the experience of it easier to bear. Remind yourself, *This is the core of the onion. It's really hard right now. It will pass, I just have to get through today.*

2. **Take a mental health day.** The core of the onion moment will likely not wait to make an appointment with you and that means that this moment may come at the most inconvenient of times. You might have a work deadline or a school exam. As much as possible or as

1 Thompson & Waltz (2010).

soon as possible, take a day off to face it. Stay in bed if you need to. Cry if you need to. But please, do not watch TV or distract yourself in any way. Just allow yourself to sit and breathe and cry. This is what healing looks like – it is messy and, just like food poisoning, the more you process it, the faster you get it out of your system.

3. **Write out your memory.** Writing out your memory and then reading it out loud can allow you to process it on a deeper level. This process can allow you to, over time, make peace with what happened to you. If you were abused or traumatised in any way, none of it was okay. This process is never meant to trivialise what happened to you. Rather, it is meant to help you cope with what happened to you – to understand that what happened to you was not okay. It is also meant to help you to face what you have been through so that it does not hold you back or taunt you any further.

4. **Break up your symptoms into separate physical components.** Just like we practised in Chapter 11, see if you can break up your symptoms into separate physical components, such as a tightness in the chest, feeling out of breath, feeling numb, tingly or shaky, or having a queasy stomach. See if you can isolate the physiological elements of what you are feeling right now. This is especially important because much of our past trauma lives in our body.[2] Being able to notice your physical sensations

2 Van der Kolk (2014).

when you are in the core of the onion moment can allow you to heal some of the lasting imprints of your past trauma. If possible, once you notice some of the physical components of your current experience, see if you can focus on them one at a time. Just like we practised in the previous chapter, see if you can sit with each sensation separately for at least two minutes while consciously breathing. The valve exercise from the previous chapter can be especially helpful here as well.

5. **Grounding.** For many of us, when we are in the core of the onion, we are either stuck in the painful past or are ruminating about a terrifying future. Some people might have terrifying intrusive thoughts playing in their minds. However, none of these thoughts are dangerous. These are thoughts that our mind produces when we are overwhelmed, triggered, or in the core of the onion. One way to help our anxiety settle is to practise grounding. A grounding exercise is one in which you can bring your attention to the present moment, while noticing and allowing the thoughts and feelings that you are experiencing. For example, you can ask yourself, 'Where are my feet?'[3] This exercise is meant to help you find an anchor to the present moment. It is meant to allow you to notice that right now, in this moment, you are safe.[4] It is a way

3 If the sensation of your feet is not available to you, you can instead focus on the sensation of your hands or the sensation of your lips.

4 If you are not physically safe, please get yourself to safety immediately before continuing with these exercises.

to notice that if in the past you went through terrible things, you are currently safe in the present moment.

6. **Reach out to someone.** If you are struggling, it is always okay to reach out to someone. If you can, please reach out to a trusted friend or a therapist. Having someone to talk to can help you to get through the core of the onion moment. At the end of the book, you can find some mental health resources for the UK and the US. If you live in another country, please write down the important numbers and websites to keep in mind, so that you have them in case of an emergency.

7. **Do something kind for yourself.** At the end of the day, after you have allowed yourself to process some of your experiences, please do something for yourself. You can watch a favourite TV show or movie, play a video game or have a soothing snack to support yourself, guilt-free. Make yourself some warm tea or hot soup to soothe your soul.

It is important to soothe and support yourself after these painful experiences to allow you to have an easier time facing them. This will likely not be the only core of the onion moment you will face and being able to soothe yourself afterward can make it easier for you to face this experience in the future.

Another helpful technique to help you practise acceptance of your past experiences is to create a timeline of your life. In this timeline, you can make a bullet point list of some of the events that happened to you. These could be challenging events, such as coping with a painful breakup, and also events in which you showed perseverance, such as walking away from an unhealthy friendship or quitting a job that wasn't suiting your needs.

Here is an example of a fictionalised timeline:

- Born in New York City
- Age 3 – parents got a divorce
- Age 3 – got a new puppy
- Age 5 – abuse from my father starts
- Age 7 – finally able to tell my mother about the abuse
- Age 8 – started to live with mother full-time
- Age 9 – met my best friend, Sarah
- Age 9 – travelled to France with mother and sister
- Age 15 – first boyfriend
- Age 16 – sexual assault, broke up with my boyfriend
- Age 16 – found out that Sarah had been assaulted too. Helped her cope
- Age 18 – got accepted at university on a full scholarship
- Age 21 – PTSD symptoms started
- Age 22 – started drinking a lot
- Age 23 – started seeing a counsellor, started getting sober and processing my trauma

In this example, the individual, let's call her 'Julia', went through several instances of abuse and trauma. She also had multiple instances of being able to stand up for herself and help others to cope with their traumatic experiences. In helping

Julia see her full timeline and being able to retell her auto-biographical story, she may have an easier time understanding and accepting what happened to her. Similar exercises are utilised in Narrative Exposure Therapy (NET) practices and have been shown to be helpful in assisting trauma survivors with accepting and managing their symptoms.[5]

Another helpful exercise in helping you cope with being at the core of the onion is the Time Travel exercise.

Time Travel exercise

Take a few moments to remember a painful event in your life, such as a past heartbreak, rejection or bullying. If this is your first time doing this exercise, please start with a mildly or moderately distressing event, as opposed to the worst event in your life.

Take a few moments to recall what happened. Remember the details of what was said, what happened and who was there.

Then, imagine that you are able to time travel – the current you, the wise you, the experienced you. See if you can travel back to that moment in which the painful event happened and see if there is anything you would say or do to comfort your younger self. Would you hug the little you? What might you say to explain what is happening and how the little you might get past it? What might be the kindest and the most compassionate thing that you can say to your little self in that moment?

5 Orang, et al. (2018).

_____

_____

_____

_____

_____

_____

_____

The purpose of this exercise is to help you, the current you, accept and understand the painful experiences you have lived through; see how challenging they truly were; and allow yourself to process, grieve and heal from them in the way that you need to.

This process is not easy. It hurts and it burns, sometimes on the inside and out. And it burns because you are a Phoenix and this is your rebirth experience. This burning will end, and you will come out on the other side, more powerful than you have ever been.

Chapter 13
Empathic Distress and Coping With Social Injustice

The first of September, 2004. That date is forever etched into my memory. In the Russian culture, September the 1st is a very important day. Like a graduation at the end of the year, September the 1st signifies children's advancement to the next grade in the beginning of the year and also celebrates children who are just starting school (first graders). It is a holiday during which all children, all parents and all teachers are in attendance. Everyone wears their best dress clothes and must bring flowers and presents for first graders. There is usually music, a marching band and speeches welcoming the children to their new adventure. The more senior students often speak words of encouragement to the younger ones, while the teachers meet the new students they will be mentoring that year.

And on September the 1st, 2004, on a beautiful sunny day, which welcomed children to the new year of their school in Beslan, Russia, an unimaginable tragedy happened. Thirty-two militants seized the school taking over 1,100 hostages, 777 of whom were children. The siege, which lasted three days, resulted in 331 deaths, more than half of which (i.e., 186) were children.

To say that I was 'glued' to the television for those three days would be an understatement. I kept replaying the news. I obsessively read all the papers that I could. I scoured the internet to find out more information. I barely saw much coverage of it on the news. It would be mentioned briefly on the nightly news, and it was mentioned in the newspapers, but most people were either not aware of the event or were not too fazed by it.

'What do you care? It's going on all the way over in Russia,' one of my friends said to me.

I couldn't sleep. I couldn't eat. I had to stay off work and missed two days of my college classes because I was so grief-stricken that I couldn't function. What made it worse was that I was the only person I personally knew that felt that way. This meant that unlike the events of 9/11, there was no one I could process this with, there was no one I could grieve or cry with; and because the tragedy happened on the other side of the world, there was no one I could help directly.

I wanted to yell at people – asking them about why they didn't care. I wanted to let out the most primal scream. I grieved. I sobbed. And I felt completely and utterly useless. I felt a pull to do something. To help in some way.

Whether it has to do with countless amounts of people that die from terrorist attacks, natural disasters, deadly pandemics, or due to racism or other forms of prejudice, dealing with this kind of pain is never easy. Seeing other people treated unjustly, learning about a loved one who was killed or sexually assaulted, or learning about an injustice happening to someone you have never met can all lead to an overwhelming amount of grief and depression, especially if you are a highly empathic person.

What's worse is that oftentimes the people in your life may not understand why you might grieve the deaths of people you have never met or why you might care about issues that might not affect you personally. Hearing others regard human tragedies in a nonchalant way can be extremely jarring for a caring and a compassionate individual.

If you are someone who feels other people's pain, if you are someone who grieves the deaths of people you have never met, if you are someone who is passionate about equality and fair treatment, then you may be a highly empathic person. Being a highly empathic person might mean that you are highly sensitive to your and other people's emotions and needs, and that you might feel strongly about the rights and wrongs of the world.

Being a highly empathic person isn't wrong. In fact, I think of it as a superpower. If you are sensitive enough to understand other people's emotions and feel their pain, then you are more likely to take steps to make a difference in this world. In fact, we know that people who are highly empathic are neurologically more wired to be attuned to other people's suffering than those who are not highly empathic. In addition, people who are highly empathic are also more likely to demonstrate the activation of the motor and planning parts of their brain, suggesting that they are more likely to plan to initiate some kind of a helpful action when witnessing other people's suffering.[1]

1 Acevedo, et al. (2014).

Being empathically tuned to feel other people's pain and taking a step toward helping that individual preserves not only their wellbeing but also our own. When we are able to help other people, by merely being kind and present, they might feel better. This, of course, doesn't mean that you will be able to completely take away someone else's pain. When we hug someone at a funeral, we don't hug them to take away their pain. We hug them *because* they are in pain. Providing this kind of support might help not only the other person but it might help us, too.[2]

Our bodies release a special hormone, *oxytocin*, when we are either supporting someone or receiving support from someone else. This hormone can help to soothe some of our deepest suffering while allowing us the resilience to show up for our pain. It is exactly why so many of us might be driven to give or receive physical comfort, such as a hug, when something bad has happened.[3] This is exactly why parents may hug their child when their child is sad or scared. For most people, when we see someone who is suffering, we want to help – we have an instinct and an inner desire to help. And our bodies are biologically pre-wired to reward us for helping by supplying us with oxytocin and other feel-good chemicals.

But what happens when we can't help? What happens when we witness the atrocities of the world, such as hundreds or thousands of people who might have died in a terrorist attack, the millions of people who died from the coronavirus pandemic, or

2 Lama (2009); Jinpa (2016).
3 Neff & McGehee (2010).

the countless amounts of lives lost on a daily basis because of racism, homophobia, transphobia or misogyny?

Being unable to help people who are suffering can be devastating, especially for those of us who are highly empathic, oftentimes leading us to experience *empathic distress* and *moral injury*. Empathic distress means that because we might empathise with other people's pain and suffering, we might feel completely depleted and highly distressed if we are unable to help them.[4] On the other hand, going through a moral injury refers to acting in a way that is contrary to our moral values or being unable to take steps that honour our core values.[5]

Just like PTSD, moral injury was previously believed only to occur in military service members, especially those who had to kill people in combat. However, nowadays, we know that just like PTSD, moral injury can occur in anyone, especially in people who are highly compassionate and those who value helping other people. For example, rates of moral injury rose at alarmingly high rates during the coronavirus pandemic because many of the doctors were unable to help all the patients that they were seeing. Hence, being unable to help someone when they are suffering can feel like an injury to ourselves. We may start thinking that anything we can do might be too small and 'won't help anyway'. As a result, we might retreat, shut down or numb out, which will usually lead to us further shaming ourselves. When we step away from helping people, we are likely to believe that we are selfish, weak or otherwise

4 Klimecki, et al. (2014); Klimecki & Singer (2012).
5 Litz, et al. (2009); Ford (2019).

a 'bad person'. And yet, nothing can be further from the truth. When we see suffering, we suffer, too, because we care. Just like hugging someone at a funeral, we may wish to help but might be too overwhelmed by the large scale of the problem, making us doubt our own capacity to help. However, your very suffering, your very distress is pushing you to help – your internal distress signal is wanting you to take action.

I lived in New York during 9/11 and I saw the Twin Towers fall in front of me. I also saw more compassion during that day, that week and that month in the city of New York than I had ever seen before. I saw people holding one another. I saw people helping each other to look for missing family members and to hand out flyers. People were lending phones to each other, giving food and water to each other, and holding each other's hands. What we know now, all these years later, is that people who helped others during a tragedy like 9/11 were less likely to develop PTSD later on. People who receive support during tragedies report lower PTSD rates as well.

On the other hand, avoidance of helping or reaching out for help, as well as avoidance of taking a step toward acting within our core values is more likely to bring on moral injury and PTSD.[6] What this means is that allowing ourselves to feel the pain of the situation and taking a step to help makes a difference both for us and for other people.

The assumption that we often have is that if we are unable to take away someone's pain or change the large picture (e.g.,

6 Nieuwsma, et al. (2015).

systemic racism), then there is nothing we can do. So, what do we do when the problem is too big and we feel too overwhelmed? What are some of the steps that we can then take? First, acknowledging how severe the problem is can be helpful in that it can allow us to realise how quickly we need to act. In some situations, the problem might be large and urgent, in which case, we may need to act quickly or even immediately.

Second, taking some time to process our own emotions about the event is crucial. Taking time to honour your own grief and anger, and noticing your own empathic distress, can help you to have an easier time responding to the event than if you attempt to numb it out or avoid it altogether.

Third, taking one step, just one step, to make a difference is not insignificant. Oftentimes, we might feel so focused on the large scale of the specific injustice that it might be hard to think about just one action. It might seem small and inconsequential. And yet, that is how the world changes. It starts with one action. It starts with you. You taking one step will lead to others taking a step, and this effect can magnify and grow over time. One voice may not bring about the kind of change you would like to see, but amplifying your voice or joining thousands of other voices will move mountains. Taking one step, such as providing information to others, fundraising or calling your representatives can start that ripple effect.

Finally, you can focus on clearly instructing other people as to the one step they can take to make a difference. Many people might be hesitant, or even defensive, when it comes to helping if they don't have a clue as to what they can do. That is when you are more likely to hear people say things like, 'What difference does it make? It's not like this action will change anything.' This apparent indifference could, in some cases, be the result of the other person's own empathic distress or moral injury that they are unable or not ready to cope with. However, when a person knows what they can do to contribute, they are likely to be more willing to try.

At times, seeing other people's pain might invigorate you to take action. At other times, it might make you want to curl into your bed and cry, or turn off the world. The latter is an example of what empathic distress feels like. Before we go into how to manage empathic distress, let's talk about how or why it happens.

Empathic distress refers to the amount of emotional energy we are putting out being greater than the emotional energy reserves we have available. In this case, what we are essentially talking about is emotional burnout. It often happens because we might not be able to recharge our energy reserves while we are exposed to a vast amount of suffering.[7]

Empathic distress can occur anywhere – at work, at home, or in any environment in which we may be expected to care for other people or are exposed to the suffering of others. In some people, empathic distress is experienced as emotional numbing to the suffering of others. Some people may become irritable, angry or anxious, and might say or think unkind things toward the people they are caring for. Some people may experience

7 Klimecki, et al. (2014).

depression, hopelessness or even suicidal thoughts, often wishing to be left alone and not wanting to be around other people.

Experiencing empathic distress doesn't mean that there is anything wrong with you. It doesn't make you selfish or unkind. Rather, it means that you are depleted and need to recharge your internal battery. It means that you are likely needing self-compassion and a break in order to fill up your own energy before you can be expected to care for others.

If you have ever flown on an airplane, you may remember the flight attendants reminding you that in case of an emergency, oxygen masks will be available to passengers, and that passengers need to secure their own oxygen mask first before they tend to others. At home, in our workplace, in school and with our friends we also need to secure our metaphorical oxygen mask first before attending to others. This need is not selfish, it is necessary. If you don't have any emotional resources left, if you are running on empty and have no energy, then you will likely have nothing to offer to help others. You taking time to recharge allows you to be better at caring for others – it allows you to be more compassionate and more resilient when it comes to witnessing other people's pain or taking care of others.[8] And the more emotionally sensitive, empathic and/or introverted you might be, the more you will likely need to recharge.

Some ways that you can recharge include:

- Physically stepping away from the situation – going for a walk, going into another space to allow yourself to

8 Klimecki, et al. (2014); Neff & Germer (2018).

breathe and take a break. The more emotionally burned out you are, the more frequent breaks you will need. The more people you are caring for or caring about, the more breaks you will need. The more it feels like you do not have time to step away, the more breaks you will need.

- Allowing yourself to feel any emotions that come up without judgement. You might feel sad, devastated, angry, frustrated or overwhelmed. Allow yourself the time and the space to feel these emotions, cry if you need to, and remind yourself that it makes sense that you are feeling the way that you are feeling. Many people in your situation would feel the same way. You are allowed to feel the way that you do, and you are allowed to take your time to be with your feelings.

- 'Bubble up' – visualise a clear bubble around you. Your own emotional energy stays inside your bubble and other people's emotional energy stays on the outside of your bubble. This visualisation exercise can allow you to have a degree of emotional separation from other people, which can serve two purposes. One, it can allow you to reduce emotional distress and burnout. Two, it can allow you to be able to see other people as separate human beings, rather than as enmeshed parts of you, allowing you to be more compassionate toward them. For example, if you are a carer for your family member, you might sometimes become extremely frustrated with them, especially if you are burned out. As a result, you may become impatient and lash out. By practising the bubble exercise, you can potentially learn to see another person as a separate human being, as someone who is suffering, someone you can feel compassionate toward, and someone you can empathise with.

- Mindfulness – breaking down your feelings in the body in the same way as we practised in Chapter 11 can help you to unwind and release some of the physical and emotional stress from your body. Focus on each physical component separately. For example, notice the sensations in your stomach, then in your chest, then in your shoulders, then in your jaw, one at a time. Breathe for a few minutes while noticing only one sensation at a time.

- Self-Compassion practices – wrap yourself in a blanket, hug a pillow or place your hands on your heart centre. All of these activities can stimulate the release of *oxytocin*, a hormone that can help us to self-soothe when we are distressed or burned out. For more information on self-compassion practices, I highly recommend Kristin Neff and Chris Germer's book, *The Mindful Self-Compassion Workbook: A Proven Way to Accept Yourself, Build Inner Strength, and Thrive.*

- Compassion cultivation practices. Compassion cultivation refers to purposely taking time to increase and strengthen your compassion muscle. This means purposely thinking of ways either to take kind actions or to offer silent thoughts or wishes of compassion to people who are going through a hard time. For example, when talking to a friend who is going through a painful breakup, we can practise silently sending them loving kindness wishes, such as 'May you be happy. May you find healing. May you find inner peace.' Alternatively, you can practise taking a breath in (inhale) to recharge your emotional energy, and taking a breath out (exhale) to send loving energy toward your friend. Such compassion cultivation practices have been shown to reduce people's empathic distress and allow us to be more present for other people's suffering.[9] If you are working on compassion cultivation, start with imagining sending compassionate wishes toward a relatively easy person, such as a dear friend, or even a pet, before working on sending compassionate wishes toward a more difficult person.

- At times when you are feeling burdened and overwhelmed, remind yourself what it is all for. For example, if you are fighting against racial injustices and you are feeling burned out, remind yourself that you are fighting for a very important cause. It is understandable that you might feel exhausted and depleted. You feel this way because you care. And taking time to recharge can mean that you can come back with more energy to support the cause that you care about.

- Take action. However big or small, take some kind of an

9 Neff & Germer (2018); Klimecki, et al. (2014).

action to help yourself and to help others. This action could be sending a silent meditation wish to the people who are suffering. It could be to share a fundraiser link on your social media. It could be having a conversation about the specific event or cause with someone you trust. No action is too small, and every action makes a difference. The more often you take actions to help other people who are going through something painful, the easier it might be to find the willingness to face some of the really painful things that you or other people have experienced.

Whenever you are feeling overwhelmed by the amount of suffering around you, remember that it's okay to take time for yourself to recharge. It is okay to take time for you because each moment that you take for yourself gives you a supercharge to come back stronger and more powerful in your ability to help others.

Chapter 14
Acceptance of Assistance

I have always been an overachiever. Like a best friend, it has been a reliable coping mechanism for my past trauma and my frequent feelings of not being good enough. And yet, no matter how much I have ever been able to achieve, my inner critic has never been satisfied, always wanting me to have worked harder, performed better and have accomplished more.

I have been battling with my neverending to-do list for most of my life. Every day, I would write out a long list of things that needed to get done and most days I would procrastinate doing them. Don't get me wrong, I would still get *some* things done. But the vast majority of the to-do items on my list would then have to be transferred to the next day's list of torture. The list has always seemed so daunting that even starting it seemed like an impossible task. When I wouldn't complete all the items on my to-do list, I was extremely critical of myself. *Lazy! Worthless! A failure!* These were just some of the things I would say to myself.

Then one day, in 2014, I had a really profound experience with my inner critic. I woke up feeling determined to tackle my to-do list once and for all. I wrote out everything that I planned to do that day – all twenty-six items. Then, I decided that I would do the math and try to figure out how much time each item would realistically take to complete before scheduling each item into my workday.

After I did the math, I realised that the items on my to-do list would take me approximately 532 hours to complete. That means just a little over three weeks, with no food, no sleep, and no time for my actual day job responsibilities. I actually laughed out loud when I saw the numbers. Here I was, being so hard on myself for failing to complete my to-do list, but never realising that I would have to invent a time machine to be able to complete it all in the amount of time that I was actually allotting for myself.

Oftentimes, we may get caught up in the productivity tidal wave as a way to hide the parts of ourselves that we falsely believe to be unacceptable. We might focus on external accomplishments while neglecting our internal needs. Don't get me wrong, there is nothing wrong with being ambitious. It is a wonderful quality, one which allows us to meet and honour our goals.

However, *the way* that we expect ourselves to achieve our goals matters. If we expect to meet all of our (often) unrealistic standards and we are unwilling to accept that most important things take time, unwilling to accept help, support, or setbacks, we are more likely to give up altogether. On the other hand, the willingness to focus on small goals, one at a time, the willingness to accept other people's help, the willingness to ask for help, or to delegate tasks can actually make it more likely for you to succeed and to bounce back from any setbacks that you may encounter along the way.

It is okay to not be okay. It is okay to play, to take time for a joyful activity, or to take time for a nap. And it is always okay to ask for help.

Acceptance of Assistance

I like to think of it in terms of spoons. According to the Spoon Theory,[1] we each start out our day with a certain number of metaphorical spoons. These 'spoons' represent how much mental and physical energy we have versus how much we have spent. For example, when you wake up fully rested in the morning, we might say that you started your day with twelve spoons. However, if you didn't get a good night of sleep, you may already be starting your day with a decreased number of available spoons, beginning your day with ten spoons as opposed to your usual twelve, for example.

If you have a fight with a friend, that might cost you two more spoons. If you have a chronic health condition, such as back pain, fibromyalgia, migraines, depression or anxiety, you may be losing one spoon every hour that you have to manage these challenging symptoms. Before you know it, you might be out of spoons by midday. And if so, it is no wonder you may not feel like doing any house chores or remaining items on your to-do list. You aren't being lazy; you are needing to rest and replenish your spoons before you can do anything else.

Think about how we treat our mobile phones. When the charge on our phone is getting low, most of us are likely to charge it to make sure that it continues to work. Well, what if we treated our bodies like our mobiles? What if we could regularly check in with ourselves to see our internal battery levels to see if we need to recharge ourselves, too?

1 Miserandino (2003).

Take a second right now, in this moment, to observe how you are feeling. To the best of your understanding, what is your spoon level right now? On a scale of zero to twelve, with zero being 'fully depleted' and twelve being 'fully restored', what is your level?

Relaxed, restored and peaceful ······ 12

··············· 11

Feeling good overall, some mild distress
or discomfort
······ 10

··············· 9

Can generally handle it, but with some effort.
Starting to feel 'a little off'
8

7

Not feeling well. Feeling edgy, irritable
or frustrated
6

5

Starting to really stress out. Feeling out of
breath or in a lot of pain, having a hard time
focusing, starting to have decision fatigue ···· 4

3

Stressing out a lot, wanting to leave or hide
2

Feeling extremely overwhelmed or numb,
can't stand things for much longer
1

Completely burned out, in a lot of physical
or emotional pain, can't complete even a
simple task, full decision fatigue
0

Acceptance of Assistance

If you are running at an eight or below, it might be time to recharge. What are some ways that you might be able to recharge or gain one or two spoons back? For example, you might need to eat, take a nap, take a walk, take a break, do a breathing exercise or get a hug. See if you can think about two or three emergency ways that you can recharge your spoons when you are running empty.

Here are some ideas:

- Allow yourself a break to take a short nap or walk away from what you are doing for a few minutes
- Eat something and drink some water
- Take a sick day (a 'recharge day' and a mental health day is just as important as taking time to recover from the flu). Take a day for the purpose of staying in bed to allow your body and your mind to rest
- Allow yourself to feel whatever you are feeling. Allow yourself to vent or to cry either with a trusted friend or by yourself
- Practise the 'Bubble Up' and mindfulness exercises from Chapter 13
- Allow yourself to accept the fact that you are a human being and you deserve rest and support just like any other person you might care about does
- Allow yourself to get the support from people you care about

Every person, real and fictional, needs friends and sidekicks sometimes. Even Superman sometimes needs the support of his fellow superheroes, the members of the Justice League, to assist him in saving the world. Like Superman, it makes sense for you, too, to turn toward your own sidekicks to assist you when you are facing some of your biggest challenges.

Sometimes our sidekicks include our friends, classmates or co-workers. Sometimes, our sidekicks might be our family members or our pets. Sometimes, they might be our chosen families – families that we have become a part of by choice, not necessarily people to whom we are related. Whoever your sidekicks are, it not only makes sense to call on them when you need them, but it is one of the most courageous and recharging actions you can take. Having a helpful person in your corner, having someone you can talk to, someone who can listen to you and offer compassion and support to you is a wonderful way to replenish your spoons.

In addition to receiving compassionate support from your sidekicks, you can also offer compassion toward your internal monsters. Our internal monsters are any thoughts, feelings, sensations or memories that we may not want to have. For example, our monsters might be our depression, anxiety, trauma reactions, our thoughts of being 'not good enough' or our physical pain. Our monsters aren't the perpetrators of abuse, but they may be the result of it. Years of past pain, oppression and trauma can sometimes lead to us abusing ourselves the way that others have abused us. One way to break this cycle of self-abuse is to practise getting to know your internal monsters and, over time, seeing if you can practise compassion toward them.

Compassion for the Monsters Exercise[2]

We are so used to assuming that our internal monsters are 'bad' and that we need to 'make them go away' that we don't often stop to think about whether those monsters are actually monsters at all. Is it perhaps possible that they are scary because we are hurt? In other words, could the monsters be a representation of an injured part of us that really needs love and healing?

Let's try a brief writing exercise. First, take a few moments to think about who your monsters are – perhaps you struggle with anxiety, depression, anger or insecurity. Think about who your monsters are and what they are typically telling you. What are some of the messages they frequently send you?

_____

_____

_____

_____

_____

_____

Next, take a moment to consider that the monsters might not be saying these things out of malice, but rather because they have some kind of an unmet need, such as the need for love, support or emotional or physical safety.

2 This exercise initially appeared in Scarlet, J. (2021) *Superhero Therapy for Anxiety and Trauma.*

What might your monsters actually need when they are behaving this way?

_____

_____

_____

_____

_____

_____

_____

_____

_____

_____

Next, take a moment to imagine that perhaps your monsters might actually be trying to protect you from something but perhaps aren't using the best strategies for doing so. For instance, your monsters could be trying to protect you from criticism from others by criticising you so harshly that no matter what anyone else says, it cannot be as painful as what your monster already says to you. Or, perhaps your monsters are trying to protect you from rejection, heartbreak or further pain? Perhaps they are trying to scare you into being 'perfect', into working hard to avoid further pain or rejection? See if you can write down some possibilities of what your monsters might be trying to protect you from.

_____

_____

_____

_____

_____

_____

_____

_____

_____

_____

_____

Now, see if you can thank the monsters for looking out for you and give them reassurance that you don't need their help at this time. For example, you can say, 'Thanks, anxiety. I know you're trying to look out for me, but I've got it from here.'

See if you can practise that in the space below:

_____

_____

_____

_____

Whatever steps you need to take care of yourself, please allow yourself to take them. There is no shame in needing a break or in asking for help. You are not broken. You are a human being. And you already broke the laws of physics just to be here. You are a courageous, compassionate and wonderful human, and your feelings are the most magical part of you.

Chapter 15
Building Boundaries

It doesn't matter how old I am, one factor remains pretty constant – when I am around my parents, I still feel like a small child.

My relationship with my parents is a complicated one. It was rocky for most of my childhood, adolescence and young adulthood. However, in the past few years, our relationship has significantly improved.

As a child, I was terrified of my mother, often worrying that she might be upset with me or punish me in some way. When she looked upset, I would often assume that she was angry with me and mentally review all our interactions to try to figure out what I did wrong. I would also engage in the fawning response,[1] a kind of people-pleasing response that can come out of trauma. I would clean my room, I would offer to do the dishes, and I would go out of my way to compliment my mother, anything to get her to not be upset.

Even as an adult in my thirties, living more than 3,000 miles away from my parents, I still worry about what my parents might think about my decisions and actions. When I was going through my divorce, the biggest thing weighing on my mind wasn't the devastation of an ended marriage, it was what

1 Walker (2013).

my parents would think and say about it. I didn't realise then how much my ability to accept myself, my life and my choices, depended on my mother's ability to accept me. It applied to my career choices, my decision not to have biological children, and to my weight gain. It applied to my divorce and my second marriage. It applied to my career choices and to my decision to adopt more than one cat. In all of these, my biggest stressor was the terror of my parents' potential lack of acceptance. In all of these, the thoughts of what my parents would say would bring me to my knees, leaving no room for acceptance or processing of my own feelings about these events.

When I got remarried, my partner and I would fly to visit my parents several times per year, always staying with them. As nice as it was to see my parents, especially given our much improved relationship in my adulthood, I always felt tense being around them. I wanted to spend time with them, and I also wanted to have a little break from them to relax and unwind because I realised that I was holding my breath whenever I was near them. As a result, our trips were both nice and very stressful at the same time.

Then, one trip changed everything.

We were planning to go to New York for one of my book signings and as always, planned to stay with my parents. I realised how much I was tensing my shoulders and clenching my jaw just thinking about it. When I brought it up with my therapist, she said, 'What would happen if you stayed in a hotel instead?'

I must have stared at her for at least two solid minutes before answering.

'You don't understand,' I finally said. 'My mother would never agree to that. My parents will never understand. In our culture, children always stay with their parents when they visit. No one EVER stays in a hotel when they are visiting the same city.'

My therapist looked at me for a few moments nodding and smiling. 'I see ... Well, just hypothetically speaking, what would happen if you decided to try it?'

I thought about it. I was anxious just thinking about it, but I did. 'My mother would never accept it.'

'And then what would happen?'

'She would put a guilt trip on me, and I would feel stressed-out and uncomfortable.'

My therapist tilted her head, and with a kind smile said, 'Correct me if I'm wrong, but aren't you always stressed-out and uncomfortable when you're around your parents?'

'Well ... yes ... I suppose.'

'Then what would be different about this?'

I was stumped. After a few minutes, I said, 'I guess nothing. I would still feel stressed and guilty, which I often do, and ... I would also have some time to decompress alone with my husband.'

I decided that I wanted to try it but was not yet ready to be fully honest with my parents, so I devised a little white lie. I told my parents that my publisher insisted that I stay in a hotel close to where the book signing would be taking place in case there were any interviews or last-minute promotional events. And since my parents lived in Brooklyn, over an hour away from the book signing, I thought it would be an easy lie to tell.

I am not in the business of telling lies. Lying makes me very uncomfortable, not to mention very ashamed. If I ever tell a 'little white lie', I tend to somehow slip up and not sound convincing. And that is exactly what happened in this case. My mother saw right through my lie and confronted me. With a guilt trip.

'I don't believe you. It's because you don't want to stay with us, isn't it?'

My heart sank. 'No, mom. That's not it . . . I . . .'

'It's because you're upset with me. I always try to be a good mother . . .'

'No, mom, it's not that, I just . . .'

'You know, one day I'm going to die and then you'll regret not having spent more time with your mother.'

There it was. One of her best weapons.

I sighed. There was a pause before I finally spoke. 'Mom, look, I love you very much. It's just easier for us to stay closer to the signing. Easier for many reasons and this is what we both want. We will still see you and dad; we will meet for several dinners. We will come see you in Brooklyn, anywhere you'd like to meet.'

'Then why not just stay with us? What will people think if they find out you're in town and you're not staying with your parents?'

'Mom, I love you. It's going to be okay. Let me know when and where you'd like to meet for dinner, and we'll see you and dad then.'

I was shaking when I got off the phone. I had four panic attacks that day and several more prior to the trip. But the trip itself was incredible. It was the most relaxed I had ever been while visiting New York. My interactions with my parents were pleasant and mindful. I was able to be more in the moment with them, as opposed to focusing on what they might be thinking about me. Being able to set that boundary and work on refilling my spoons (see Chapter 14 for review of the Spoon Theory) by staying in a hotel with my partner allowed me to have a more mindful and meaningful relationship with my parents.

By accepting the discomfort that came with setting a boundary, I was actually able to take a bigger step toward improving my relationship with them than when I was fawning over them. And you know what else? Having some distance from my parents allowed me the chance to process some of the complexities of our relationship. It allowed me to grieve over the relationship we didn't have and also allowed me to recognise the caring and supportive things that my parents had done for me over the years. Our relationship is by no means perfect but after setting that boundary, it became better than it had been before. And for that, I am grateful.

For some of us, boundary setting might be fairly manageable and for some, it might be extremely challenging. In some situations, boundary setting may seem relatively easy, while in other situations it may seem impossible. Whether you are facing a conflict with a family member, a friend, a boss or even with yourself, boundary setting can allow you and any other parties involved a chance to cool off and 'zoom out' from the way that each of you sees the situation.

When we are too 'zoomed in', when we are too close to a

certain situation, a feeling, or a work of art, we might have a rather skewed perspective of it. When we are able to 'zoom out' and take a step back, we might be more objective and skilful in the way we approach that situation. Hence, setting a boundary isn't a violation, it is a necessity that can allow all parties involved to have the best chance of being heard and understood when the boundary is honoured.

Boundary setting can be accomplished in a number of different ways, such as making a request, taking a break from a person, situation or phone/email messages. Boundary setting can also include saying 'no' to a specific activity, request, expectation or an assignment. Here are some ways to practise setting boundaries:

Firstly, by making requests. When people do something that hurts or upsets us, they frequently don't realise the impact of their actions. That is, unless we tell them. Of course, doing so is easier said than done. Oftentimes, we might be so scared about saying something or doing something to upset or offend the other person that we might avoid opening up to them about how we feel, suppressing our feelings on the matter, until we are fed up. Then, we might explode from the harboured resentment, while the other person might be surprised by our reaction and is likely to get hurt or become defensive. Avoidance of boundary-setting or passive hinting at what your needs are is likely to be misunderstood by the other person. This can potentially lead to a later conflict, the very thing you were probably hoping to avoid by not setting a boundary in the first place.

So then, what are some of the steps that you can take to set a boundary with another person in terms of making a request so that they change their behaviour? Let's imagine a situation in which your co-worker listens to the radio in the office, which causes you to have a hard time concentrating. Perhaps, you have tried sighing, rolling your eyes, walking away or putting on your noise-cancelling headphones, but your co-worker just doesn't get the hint and keeps listening to the radio anyway. One day, when you are on an important work-related phone call, your co-worker's radio is interfering with you being able to maintain the important conversation you are having. After you hang up, you blow up at your co-worker and storm out. Your co-worker may be confused as they had not realised that they were doing something that was bothering you and they might also be angry with you for shouting at them.

In order to avoid such conflicts and to practise making requests, it's important to first step away and unwind until you feel well enough to approach your co-worker and ask them to set up a time to meet with you to discuss an important work-related issue. When discussing the issue, it's important to be careful to state that a person's specific actions (as opposed to the person themselves) are making you feel a certain way.

Sometimes, we might say, 'You're always driving me mad and I can't concentrate because of you! Why do you always have to listen to that damn radio at work?' There are three easily fixable mistakes in this statement.

One, this statement uses accusatory language by stating '**You're** making me feel a certain way' and 'I can't concentrate **because of you**,' as opposed to the less accusatory way of pointing out a specific problematic action, such as, '**Your playing the radio at work** is making it hard for me to concentrate.'

Two, it uses the overgeneralised word, 'always'. Words like 'always' and 'never' tend to be highly destructive in arguments. Instead, focus on specific instances. For example, you might say, '**When** you listen to your radio at work, it makes it hard for me to concentrate.'

Three, 'Why' questions often tend to come across as accusatory and shaming, even if that isn't how you intended them to sound. Instead of asking 'why' questions, focus on asking for a solution – make a specific request. This last step is the most important, and one that most people forget. When all we do is state what bothers us, the other person may feel attacked and defensive. However, making a request makes the situation fixable and the other person might be more likely to oblige.

Setting a healthy boundary in this case could look like this:

1. Stepping away from the office (e.g., going to the restroom, your car or outside) to unwind for a few minutes and cool off
2. Decide what your needs are
3. Approach your co-worker and ask them when they can meet with you for a few minutes
4. When you are both able to meet, let your co-worker know that a specific **action** (playing the radio at work) is causing you to **feel** a specific way (distracted, overwhelmed, stressed out, etc.)
5. **The most important step: Make your request.** For

example, ask your co-worker if they could use headphones to listen to the radio or not listen to it around you, or lower the volume

Here is another example. Say that whenever you feel anxious or depressed, your friend tells you to 'look at the positive' and that 'other people have it worse'. If this kind of a response is not helpful for you (most people find such comments rather unhelpful), then it might make sense to practise setting a boundary with your friend. Here is an example of the steps you could take:

1. Stepping away (e.g., going for a walk or stepping out to the restroom) to unwind for a few minutes and cool off
2. Decide what your needs are in this situation
3. Approach your friend and ask them when you can talk with them for a few minutes
4. When you are both able to talk, let your friend know that when they tell you to 'look at the positive' and that 'other people have it worse' you feel (sad, ashamed, frustrated, etc.)
5. **Make your request.** For example, 'I know you are trying to help me. It would be most helpful for me if you just asked me how you can help or just listened to me talk about how I feel. These actions actually help me to feel better over time and make me feel supported when I'm going through a hard time'

Some people might be understanding about your requests and will at least attempt to honour them. They won't always be perfect, they might slip up or forget, and it is okay to remind them of your needs.

However, other people might get defensive, or even blame you for how you feel. When your needs are consistently not being met, when you feel attacked by the other person, it is okay to take a break from your conversation with them. In fact, stepping away from a heated argument can allow all parties to cool off and think about the situation and, hopefully, have a more peaceful conversation thereafter.

When taking a break during an argument, especially during an argument with a close friend, family member or a romantic partner, it is important to specify that you are taking a break and for how long. For example, you could say, '*Okay, we are both upset right now, I am going to take a 30-minute walk, and then I will come back and we can continue this conversation.*'

Not stating the parameters of the break and just storming out will likely escalate the situation as it can make the other person feel abandoned. This will actually prevent the other person from being able to cool off while you are taking your break. In that situation, when you return, the conflict might become worse because the other person was feeling abandoned, hurt and overwhelmed.

So, in order to set a boundary during a conflict or a disagreement, consider the following steps:

1. Let the person know what is happening. For example, you can say, 'I am going for a walk', or 'I am going to

get off the phone now', or 'I am going to step away to another room'.

2. Let the person know the amount of time you will be away and when you will be back. For example, 'I am going to hang up the phone now and I am going to cool off for 30 minutes.'

3. Assure the person that when you come back, you will continue this conversation, so that they know that they will still get a chance to talk to you about what is going on. For example, 'When I come back, we can continue this conversation and hopefully then we will both be able to listen and support each other.'

Setting a boundary by taking a break from a heated or stressful discussion can be anxiety-provoking and overwhelming. And in many situations, it is also worth it. By stepping away to cool off, you and the other person can both reduce the urgency of the situation, allowing you both a better chance to be really heard and understood.

The issue with feeling the pressure of urgency is that it creates mental blinders, narrowing our worldview and not allowing us to listen to the other person, as well as not allowing us to communicate in a kind and skilful manner. When we feel the urgency to solve the problem right away or by a certain deadline, we give up our ability to listen with empathy. We give up our ability to search for solutions in a creative way. When we give into this *urgency response*, we have already lost the very compromise we were trying to find.

By taking some time away from the discussion, you can reflect on what you are trying to say and what the other person might be trying to say. It can be helpful to make a bullet-point list of the points you want to get across and also of what you think the other person might be trying to get across. When you are back in a conversation with the other individual, you can take turns comparing notes to see if you understood them correctly, if they understood you correctly, and you can both go over some of the points you are trying to get across.

Acceptance is a vital skill in managing disagreements and conflicts because it requires the acceptance of (i.e., the willingness to sit with) the discomfort of taking a break, the discomfort of the urgency response, and the discomfort of possibly being not fully heard or understood in that moment. And the more willing you are to make room for that discomfort in the service of possibly having a clearer and more empathic communication with the other person, the more likely you both are to be able to understand each other, even if you don't end up agreeing with one another.

In addition to taking a break to reduce the urgency response, other ways of setting boundaries include not responding right away to a text message, phone call or email. When you need to take a break from responding for a significant amount of time, it can sometimes be helpful to let the other individual know that you will respond to them later on. For example, you could send a message along the lines of, 'Thank you for your message. I have received it and will respond to you tomorrow.' Of course, you can also say that you will respond next week or as soon as you are able.

Letting other people know that you will respond at a later time can potentially reduce the urgency response for you and for the other party. In some instances, if the other person continues to put the pressure on you to respond earlier than your set time frame, it is okay for you not to respond to their messages until the deadline you have set. And if you need additional time, it is okay for you to let that individual know your new timeline.

Finally, another option for boundary setting is saying 'no'. This could mean not agreeing to take on an additional assignment at work, stating that you cannot help a friend with a specific situation, or stating that you cannot do something that you have previously agreed to do. If you are an overachieving, people-pleasing perfectionist like me, you may find this last type of boundary-setting to be the most cringe-worthy. And it makes sense that you might feel this way.

If you are someone who used to be punished for refusing to do something you couldn't do or were strongly opposed to doing in the past, you might be understandably uncomfortable with saying 'no' in the present, whether or not you are in danger of harsh punishment in your current circumstance. People with a history of abuse, assault or abandonment are most likely to struggle with this type of boundary-setting. That is exactly why this practice can be essential in finding your voice and helping you to restore your mental and physical energy.

If you are running out of spoons, need some time to unwind, and cannot help your friend with a problem they are having; if you are overburdened at work and cannot take on any more assignments; if your family member asks you for help when you are in a lot of pain, it is okay to say that you are unable to help them in that moment. It is okay to let that person know that you are overwhelmed and need a break, and it is also okay not to give someone a reason for why you are saying 'no'.

In some cases, when you set a boundary, the other person will understand. In other cases, they might get angry, defensive or become insulting. In those cases, boundary-setting is even more important. Oftentimes, people who get their needs met through an aggressive response (yelling, threatening, insulting or pushing) learn that so long as they push hard enough, they will get their way. If you give in when the other person is behaving in this way, you are essentially telling them that their behaviour is acceptable and that when they yell, push or insult you enough, you will give them everything they ask for. In a sense, you are reinforcing their bad behaviour, making it more likely to happen in the future.

If, however, you say 'no', one of two things will happen: either the other person will understand or they will initially protest. Protesting behaviour is common when someone is used to getting their way. But the truth is that protesting behaviour doesn't last. Like a thunderstorm, it's loud and scary in the moment, but if you can wait it out, it passes.

If you can stick to your boundary, the other person will likely reduce the pressure and will reduce how much they are pushing you over time. If you are able to keep your boundary firm, you might even develop a more autonomous and respectful relationship with that person because they may learn that when you say 'no', you mean it, and they will likely start respecting your boundaries. Alternatively, if they continue their toxic and unhelpful patterns over time, your boundaries can allow you the space to evaluate your choices to see if you still wish to associate with that individual. No matter who that person is to you – a friend, a family member, a boss or a co-worker – you never have to put up with abuse and you are never obligated to stay in contact with people who constantly hurt you.

Boundary-setting practices aren't easy. They take time and practice. If saying 'no' is too challenging to do at first, it is perfectly okay to try a *mental rehearsal* exercise. In a mental rehearsal, you would imagine having a conversation with the other person. Imagine setting a boundary with them. Imagine what they might say and do, and then imagine how you might respond. What kind of a boundary might you set if this individual does or says something hurtful? Most people might be so afraid of the other person saying something insulting to them that they never even think or plan what they might say next. By practising a mental rehearsal exercise, you can be prepared for setting a boundary even if you feel uncomfortable in the moment. By making room for the discomfort that you feel in the mental rehearsal, by building the willingness to speak your truth, even if you feel anxious, you might be more likely to practise boundary setting in real life.

Boundary-setting essentially allows you the space that you need to heal, to grow and to restore your mental and physical energy. This space can allow you to process what you are feeling so that you can see things in their full complexities. Like a painting, our emotions need some space to grow, to allow us to see their full image as opposed to when we are standing too close to make sense of them. By taking a break from a painful situation, argument or a person who wears you out, you can have more mental space to figure out how you would like to proceed. You never owe anyone an explanation for why you need to set a boundary, and even if the other person doesn't agree with you it doesn't mean that you shouldn't set it. You deserve to have your safe emotional space to breathe, to think, to figure things out, to unwind and to reload your spoons. So, go ahead, bubble up, take your space – you are allowed, and you do not ever need anyone's permission to do so.

Chapter 16
Finding YOUR Voice

Have you ever felt strongly about something only to find that the people closest to you felt the opposite way? Whether it is regarding the #MeToo movement, the Black Lives Matter movement, equality, social justice, animal rights, global or interpersonal issues, we are all allowed our own individual voices.

Acceptance here would refer to our willingness to use your voice even when it contradicts the opinions of those around you. Whether it is being authentic about our sexual orientation, our gender identity, our worldview or our life choices, it can be intimidating to use our voice to let other people know our truth.

Certain people might not ever see things from your point of view, but that doesn't make you wrong. Some people might not accept you for who you are but that doesn't mean that they are right.

Many people live in 'boxes'; they expect to have a specific linear trajectory for life. They might have set expectations for how people should be, and how people should feel and do things. This may mean that they may not understand you wanting to take a step out of the box, to colour outside of the box, and to live outside of the box.

And while some people belong in boxes, other people do not. Maybe you are not a box kind of a person. Maybe you are a unicorn, and unicorns definitely do not belong in boxes. This means that who you are, how you feel and what you do is your truth and no one else gets to tell you how to live your life. Your truth doesn't have to be the same truth as that of your family, friends or people in your immediate circle. It isn't your job to convince others to see things from your perspective and you might not be able to convince people to feel the same way you do.

Your using your voice to speak up for your truth might even be one of your core values. Core values are your life principles that allow you to live your most meaningful and authentic life. Core values may include the roles that you play, such as being a parent, a friend or a partner, for example. Your core values might also include the ways in which you wish to interact with the world and the way you uphold your own standards, in terms of loyalty, honour, authenticity or kindness. Your core values might also include categories that give your life meaning, such as creativity, travel, volunteering, speaking up for equality, etc. Your core values are different from your goals. Whereas goals are finite (for example, volunteering at an animal shelter on Saturdays), your core values are indefinite (for example, helping animals).[1]

In many ways, acceptance can be an important component of your core values. For example, by practising acceptance of your feelings and acceptance of yourself, you might be honouring the core value of authenticity. By using your voice to speak up for what you believe in or by setting boundaries with others, you may be honouring your core values of social justice and self-care.

1 Hayes, et al. (2011).

This might mean that when you are practising acceptance, you experience anxiety, flashbacks and emotional or physical pain. But it doesn't mean that these sensations are wrong. Sometimes, as we start to face our inner truth, anxiety and other emotional discomfort might show up as yet another way of peeling our inner onion. Instead of turning away from these sensations, we can turn toward them. We can ask ourselves, 'Am I willing to experience this discomfort if it means that I am able to be more authentic with myself; if I am able to have more time for myself; if I am able to stand up for what I believe in?' If the answer to any of these questions is 'yes', then perhaps we need not focus on avoiding the discomfort, but rather on honouring your core values; on honouring YOUR voice and YOUR identity regardless of any possible discomfort that you might feel in the moment.

You might recall the top five regrets of the dying we discussed in Chapter 10. By using your voice, by taking actions to honour who you are and what you stand for, even if it makes you uncomfortable, even if others don't agree with you, you are more likely to live your life with no regrets at all.

Here, when we are talking about practising acceptance, I am referring to awakening the Phoenix, the warrior inside of you. Those very feelings of anxiety that you feel – your racing heart, your breathlessness – those are exactly what we feel in moments of our greatest joy and courage.[2] It means that we don't need to avoid our physiological responses. Your thundering heart is

2 McGonigal (2016).

here to help you to distribute the blood to the vital organs of your body in order to help you be more courageous and present in this moment. Your lungs are taking in more oxygen in this moment and your racing mind is preparing you for your own heroic moment. This one.

So, if possible, try a heroic pose. Whether sitting or standing, see if you can put your arms at your sides like a superhero. Like Wonder Woman or Superman does. This kind of power posing can actually give you a little boost of confidence when you are planning on doing something challenging, such as setting a boundary or giving a talk.[3] And like a superhero, you are allowed to feel however you feel, and be who you are and what you stand for. Your anxiety, your fear, your anger, they are here to remind you of what matters most to you. This might mean having difficult conversations or it might mean pulling back from certain connections that are no longer serving you. It is okay for you to speak up for yourself even if others don't agree with you. Every action that you take to honour your core values is a heroic step forward. Allowing yourself to feel uncertain, scared, angry or uncomfortable is perfectly okay, as is taking some time to recharge and replenish your spoons.

And what if your entire life has led you right here, to this very moment? Who would you say you are, if you are the only person who gets to define you? If we assume that your voice truly makes a difference, and I truly believe that it does, then how would you like to use your voice to stand up for what you believe in?

3 Cuddy, et al. (2012).

Chapter 17
Overcoming Obstacles and Setbacks

Every hero's journey has truly triumphant moments. And every hero's journey has setbacks and obstacles along the way. Obstacles are any challenges that might come up that interfere with your plans. For example, if you were planning to meet a friend for coffee in the morning but suddenly got a flat tyre on your car. Alternatively, setbacks refer to a temporary resurgence of unhelpful behaviours. For example, if you used to rely on alcohol to help you avoid feeling painful emotions but have been sober (or have been only having a couple of occasional social drinks) for the past five weeks, then had eights drinks in a row because you had a really rough day, that would be a setback.

There is nothing wrong with enjoying having a glass of wine, a beer or another beverage once in a while. What matters is the *why*. If we are using alcohol purely to run away from a particular emotion or memory, then any potential emotion-dampening effects that alcohol might provide in the moment are likely to backfire later.

Obstacles and setbacks are both normal and expected. We all have them and we all may feel frustrated when they come up. The most important thing to remember is not to punish yourself for going through them. The truth is that facing setbacks is not a failure, but rather it is the foundation of your resilience building. If everything was easy you couldn't possibly grow and learn from it. There is no one, and I repeat, *no one on the entire planet*, that never meets obstacles and setbacks. We all face challenges on our journey, and we all sometimes slide back toward behaviours that used to reduce our painful experiences in the moment.

In my case, my unhelpful coping behaviours include having desserts that I am allergic to. I have several food allergies, including dairy and gluten, none of which are life-threatening but all of which cause stomach aches, severe joint pain and swelling and headaches for days after consuming a particular allergen-containing food. For example, butter croissants, cheesecake and coffee-flavoured ice cream are some of the things I crave after a long, hard day.

There is absolutely nothing wrong with having tasty treats and enjoying food, but in my case, my subsequent allergic reaction would make me feel very sick after eating some of my favourite desserts. Sometimes, I fall into a vicious cycle in which I want so badly to feel better after experiencing a painful trigger, or after a conflict with a family member, or after a bad bout of depression, that I crave the very desserts that my body cannot accept or process.

For me specifically, eating one of those treats allows me to temporarily suppress my depression or trauma memories. In fact, I might even feel ecstatic in the moment. However, approximately 30 minutes after consuming the dessert, my hands begin to swell and my joints feel as if they are being crushed. My stomach hurts and my whole body feels hurt and swollen. My short-term bliss leads to three or four days of physical and mental hurt. Worse, when I eat food containing my trigger allergens, it impedes my stomach's ability to produce serotonin (a chemical that is responsible for our mood, appetite and many other functions) meaning that it can actually exacerbate my depression and anxiety.

The stomach produces about 95 per cent of the body's serotonin,[1] which means that if our stomach is not functioning well, its ability to produce serotonin might temporarily reduce, causing us to feel anxious, depressed and numb. If we are also having thoughts like, 'What is wrong with me? Why did I have ice cream yesterday? I should know better!' along with some body-shaming statements (which tend to happen for me), we are likely to fall into the shame spiral. In my case, sometimes I've said things like, 'Well, f*@k it! I've already slid off my health plan, I might as well go all out.' In those instances, I might again eat the kind of dessert that can make me feel physically sick and emotionally depressed the next day, once again restarting that vicious cycle of self-criticism and pain.

The spiral here includes both obstacles and setbacks. In this example, my obstacles might be the lack of self-care or emotional support, running out of spoons and being burned out or triggered. In some instances, those obstacles can lead to setbacks, in my case, eating foods that hurt my body and make me feel worse the next day. The reason why I wanted to share

1 Carpenter (2012).

this is because we all go through obstacles and setbacks that we might feel ashamed about. The more we talk about them, the more we can do something about those feelings. And if you go through something similar, I want you to know that you aren't alone and that these setbacks and obstacles don't go on forever. They are both expected and normal. By noticing that we are having a setback, we can remind ourselves that we need some extra support and that we can always get back on track with our self-care and acceptance skills.

Some people make the assumption that progress should be linear, meaning that you should continue to use your skills and get better and better every day, like this:

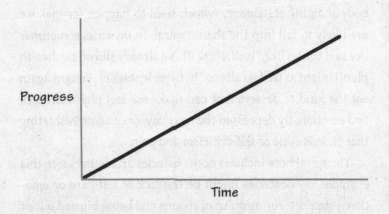

In reality, such a linear trend is neither the expectation nor the norm. Most people go through regular ups and downs in their progress, with frequent setbacks and challenges along the way, like this:

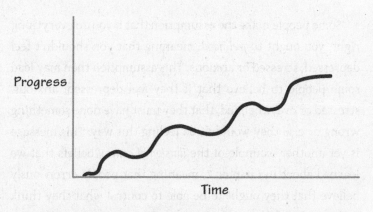

Such ups and downs are not only normal, they are necessary. It isn't helpful to always advance without any setbacks because then we never have the opportunity to learn how to face them and how to grow with them. That's right: rather than growing *from* the setbacks, we can grow *with* them. We can make space for them, remembering that your setbacks are as much a part of your personal hero's journey as your step-ups.

Setbacks are normal and a part of my routine. What helps me is naming it, normalising it, and then making an action plan. Here are some examples in case you find them helpful:

Name it: *I am experiencing a setback right now.*

Normalise it: *Setbacks are normal and common. Everyone experiences setbacks. It's how we learn to get back up that matters.*

Make an action plan: *I am going to take some time to decompress and care for myself. I will likely not feel well physically and emotionally for the next few days, so I am going to allow myself the time and the support that I need to heal. I am going to allow myself to feel what I feel, I am going to make space for any emotions that come up, and be kind and patient with myself to the best of my ability.*

Some people make the assumption that if you do everything right, you ought to *feel good*, meaning that you shouldn't feel depressed, stressed or anxious. This assumption then may lead some people to believe that if they feel depressed, anxious, stressed or overwhelmed, that they must have done something wrong or else they wouldn't be feeling this way. This message is yet another example of the *illusion of control* beliefs that we learned about in Chapter 2, meaning that people erroneously believe that they ought to be able to control what they think and how they feel.

And yet, as we know, our thoughts and our emotions are not things we can control. Not really. And when we already don't feel well, someone else's statement about how we should or should not feel brings up shame on top of the pain we are already going through. We are told that we shouldn't feel a certain way but perhaps it is the society that shouldn't *be* a certain way.

So, if you feel angry, frustrated, confused or overwhelmed, good! Use it. Use your anger as a way to stand up to oppression – your own and other people's. Use your anxiety and your depression as a gentle reminder that you need self-compassion and time to replenish your spoons, and to remind yourself of what is most important to you.

There will be multiple times in your life when you will not feel motivated, whether that lack of motivation refers to your mental health practices, your health activities, your work, or other situations. Do not wait for motivation for it may not come. Do not wait to 'feel good' before doing something that is meaningful to you. Remember that emotions follow actions, not the other way around. This means that even if you feel anxious, but you would like to practise setting boundaries with your friends or family members, you don't have to wait to feel 'more confident'. You can be anxious *AND* take action at the same time. This is the biggest core of acceptance practice: to be willing to feel anything that comes up AND to take action toward what is most meaningful to you.

Since we know that we can expect setbacks, and that setbacks and obstacles are a common part of anyone's hero's journey, it may be helpful to have a plan for how you might be able to cope with your setbacks when (not if, but when) they show up.

When I have a setback, it might look like this:

_____

_____

_____

_____

_____

_____

When I have a setback, I will focus on reviewing and practising these skills:

_____

_____

_____

It is always okay to take breaks from your work, your responsibilities and even from your goals, especially if you are feeling overwhelmed. It is okay to take time just for you. And in case there are any setbacks, it is also important to take time to come back to your overall goals and core values in a compassionate and shame-free way. Your setbacks are another opportunity to learn, to grow and to practise your skills. In other words, your setbacks and obstacles are important teachers in your journey. All of the practices we are mentioning here are just that – practices. This is not a test. It is a lifelong practice and just by trying it, you are already succeeding.

If you have ever read about any fictional heroes, like Batman for example, you might recall that these heroes face obstacles each and every day. Batman gets up every single day knowing that he will be faced with new challenges and have unexpected setbacks, too. And because he still shows up when it is most crucial, because even when he faces setbacks he still returns, that is why we care about his adventures. That is the kind of hero that we want to see on TV. That is the kind of hero that we want to look up to.

Well, the truth is, Batman isn't that different from you. You also get up every day to face numerous obstacles along the way. And just like Batman, you show up when it is really important.

Just like any superhero, you may get discouraged or frustrated along the way, you may lose faith in yourself. But the truth of the matter is that you are a goddamn hero. You have been through more than you can probably say, more than you can probably comprehend. And you are tirelessly working to learn, to grow, to help make this world a better place. Remember who you are. Remember what you stand for. The rest might be messy, as it is supposed to be. And that is also how it all falls into place.

Chapter 18
Your Phoenix Moment

From the illusion of control to 'not good enough', we all have our narratives, most of them centred around searching for the missing pieces of ourselves, searching for wholeness, searching for acceptance. But what if you didn't have to search anymore? What if I were to tell you that you have found it. Here. Right now.

You are already perfect. Exactly the way that you are. Everything you have ever shamed yourself for, anything you have ever been shamed over, anything you have ever tried to hide about who you are, about who you *truly are*, is actually the most lovable, most wonderful part of you. So, what if acceptance in this case meant the acceptance that you might not always *feel* good enough, you may not always say or do the right thing, but that you are also already perfect. What if the most perfect being is not one who, like an android from a science-fiction film, feels nothing and always makes precise and careful, calculating steps? What if the most perfect being is like a sweet little kitten or a puppy that might chase a toy, sometimes falling over in that endearing and adorable way that kittens and puppies do?

We might smile when watching children learning to walk and when watching butterflies feed on blossom nectar. Like an art piece, each of these beings are perfect in every way, both when they take steps and when they fall down. What if this kind of art-like beauty, the most awe-like sense of love and endearment, was directed toward you? What if there is already nothing you need to do to earn being loved and accepted because you already are? In every way. And yes, even now, when you might be doubting yourself. Now, when you might cry, laugh or smile. And now, when you might recall how others have treated you. And also now, when you might doubt that you are worth it. And now. Especially now – you are perfect. With everything that you are, with every part of you.

We spend most of our lives trying to fit into someone else's narrative, trying to be seen in someone else's story but the truth is that you are already the main hero in yours. And only you get to define your narrative. Only you get to tell your own story. This is your Phoenix moment.

You might recall from Chapter 4 that a Phoenix is a magical bird, said to come from the sun. A Phoenix goes through painful changes every once in a while. After the Phoenix has gone through a change, it bursts into burning flames and then falls to ash. But then the Phoenix rises again, stronger than before.

In fact, sometimes our experiences, be they trauma, anxiety or heartbreak, might make us feel like we are on fire. But like a Phoenix, we can then rise from the ashes, stronger than before.

Now, that Phoenix is you. You are here. You have arrived at this moment – the time to turn your story into your survivor story. Everything you have experienced and have been through has led you to this moment.

Your Phoenix Moment

I would like to invite you to think about yourself as a super-hero, as a Phoenix rising from the ashes, as a survivor, looking back to see how far you have come, and everything you have learned and overcome. You can also mention what you might have realised or learned as a result of this experience, as well as your sense of purpose.

If you are willing, please write out your Phoenix survivor story either in the space below or on your own page.

_____

_____

_____

_____

_____

_____

_____

_____

_____

_____

_____

_____

_____

_____

_____

_____

_____

_____

_____

_____

_____

_____

How did that feel?

Please know that your story is your truth. Who you are is your truth and you are allowed to be you. You have purpose. You bring a value to this world, more than you can possibly know. There are probably multiple people who have already been helped by something kind that you did or said to them, but they might never think to tell you about the wonderful impact you have had on their lives. There might be someone out there, who is alive today because of you, and you might never fully know just how meaningful your actions and your kindness has been. So, from the bottom of my heart, thank you for being wonderful.

And if possible, maybe take a moment to imagine taking a hero's posture with your arms at your sides or a similar position. Perhaps imagine yourself in a hero's outfit, as if to say, 'I am a Phoenix. And I have awakened.'

References

Acevedo, B. P., Aron, E. N., Aron, A., Sangster, M. D., Collins, N., & Brown, L. L. (2014). The highly sensitive brain: an fMRI study of sensory processing sensitivity and response to others' emotions. *Brain and Behavior*, 4(4), 580–594.

Benson, L. (2006). Ambiguous loss, number of foster care placements, child age and child sex as the predictors of the behaviour problems and posttraumatic stress symptoms of children in foster care (Doctoral dissertation).

Betz, G., & Thorngren, J. M. (2006). Ambiguous loss and the family grieving process. *The Family Journal*, 14(4), 359–365.

Boss, P. (2006). *Loss, trauma, and resilience: Therapeutic work with ambiguous loss.* WW Norton & Company.

Bowirrat, A., & Oscar-Berman, M. (2005). Relationship between dopaminergic neurotransmission, alcoholism, and reward deficiency syndrome. American Journal of Medical Genetics Part B: *Neuropsychiatric Genetics*, 132(1), 29–37.

Brown, B. (2015). *Daring greatly: How the courage to be vulnerable transforms the way we live, love, parent, and lead.* New York, NY: Penguin.

Carpenter, S. (2012). That gut feeling. *American Psychological Association*, 43(8), 50.

Chugani, H. T., Behen, M. E., Muzik, O., Juhász, C., Nagy, F., &

Chugani, D. C. (2001). Local brain functional activity following early deprivation: a study of postinstitutionalized Romanian orphans. *Neuroimage, 14*(6), 1290–1301.

Coan, J. A., Schaefer, H. S., & Davidson, R. J. (2006). Lending a hand: Social regulation of the neural response to threat. *Psychological Science, 17*(12), 1032–1039.

Cuddy, A. J., Wilmuth, C. A., & Carney, D. R. (2012). *The benefit of power posing before a high-stakes social evaluation.* Harvard Business School working paper series #13-027.

Dindo, L., Van Liew, J. R., & Arch, J. J. (2017). Acceptance and commitment therapy: a transdiagnostic behavioral intervention for mental health and medical conditions. *Neurotherapeutics, 14*(3), 546–553.

Ford, E. W. (2019). Stress, burnout, and moral injury: the state of the healthcare workforce. *Journal of Healthcare Management, 64*(3), 125–127.

Friedmann, E., Thomas, S. A., Liu, F., Morton, P. G., Chapa, D., & Gottlieb, S. S. (2006). Sudden Cardiac Death in Heart Failure Trial (SCD-HeFT) Investigators. Relationship of depression, anxiety, and social isolation to chronic heart failure outpatient mortality. *American Heart Journal, 152*(5), 940-e1.

Hancock, L., & Bryant, R. A. (2020). Posttraumatic stress, stressor controllability, and avoidance. *Behaviour Research and Therapy, 128*, 103591.

Hayes, S. C. (2005). *Get out of your mind and into your life: The new acceptance and commitment therapy.* Oakland, CA: New Harbinger Publications.

Hayes, S. C., Strosahl, K. D., & Wilson, K. G. (2011). *Acceptance* and commitment therapy: The process and practice of mindful change. New York, NY: Guilford Press.

Higa, K. T., Mori, E., Viana, F. F., Morris, M., & Michelini, L. C. (2002). Baroreflex control of heart rate by oxytocin in the solitary-vagal complex. *American Journal of Physiology-Regulatory, Integrative and Comparative Physiology, 282*(2), R537-R545.

Jinpa, T. (2016). *A fearless heart: How the courage to be compassionate can transform our lives.* Avery.

Kemp, A. H., Quintana, D. S., Kuhnert, R. L., Griffiths, K., Hickie, I. B., & Guastella, A. J. (2012). Oxytocin increases heart rate variability in humans at rest: implications for social approach-related motivation and capacity for social engagement. *PloS One, 7*(8), e44014.

Klimecki, O. M., Leiberg, S., Ricard, M., & Singer, T. (2014). Differential pattern of functional brain plasticity after compassion and empathy training. *Social Cognitive and Affective Neuroscience, 9*(6), 873-879.

Klimecki, O., & Singer, T. (2012). Empathic distress fatigue rather than compassion fatigue? Integrating findings from empathy research in psychology and social neuroscience. In B. Oakley, A. Knafo, G. Madhavan, & D. S. Wilson (Eds.), *Pathological Altruism*, (pp. 368-383). New York, NY: Oxford University Press.

Lama, D. (2009). *The art of happiness: A handbook for living.* Penguin.

Litz, B. T., Stein, N., Delaney, E., Lebowitz, L., Nash, W. P., Silva, C., & Maguen, S. (2009). Moral injury and moral repair in war veterans: A preliminary model and intervention strategy. *Clinical Psychology Review, 29*(8), 695-706.

McGonigal, K. (2016). *The upside of stress: Why stress is good for you, and how to get good at it.* New York, NY: Penguin.

Miserandino, C. (2003). *The spoon theory. But You Don't Look Sick.* Retrieved from https://balanceanddizziness.org/pdf/TheSpoonTheory.pdf

Neff, K., & Germer, C. (2018). *The Mindful Self-Compassion Workbook: A Proven Way to Accept Yourself, Build Inner Strength, and Thrive.* Guilford Publications.

Neff, K. D., & McGehee, P. (2010). Self-compassion and psychological resilience among adolescents and young adults. *Self and Identity, 9*(3), 225–240.

Nieuwsma, J., Walser, R., Farnsworth, J., Drescher, K., Meador, K., & Nash, W. (2015). Possibilities within acceptance and commitment therapy for approaching moral injury. *Current Psychiatry Reviews, 11*(3), 193–206.

Orang, T., Ayoughi, S., Moran, J. K., Ghaffari, H., Mostafavi, S., Rasoulian, M., & Elbert, T. (2018). The efficacy of narrative exposure therapy in a sample of Iranian women exposed to ongoing intimate partner violence—a randomized controlled trial. *Clinical Psychology & Psychotherapy, 25*(6), 827–841.

Rostila, M., Saarela, J., & Kawachi, I. (2013). Mortality From Myocardial Infarction After the Death of a Sibling: A Nationwide Follow-up Study From Sweden. *Journal of the American Heart Association, 2*(2), e000046.

Scarlet, J. (2016). Emotion Data. In Langley, T. (Ed), *Star Trek Psychology.* Sterling Press.

Scarlet, J. (2020). *Super-Women: Superhero Therapy for Women*

Battling Depression, Anxiety and Trauma. London: UK: Hachette UK.

Scarlet, J. (2021). *Superhero Therapy for Anxiety and Trauma: A Professional Guide with ACT and CBT-Based Activities and Worksheets for All Ages.* London, UK: Jessica Kingsley Publishers.

Schimpff, S. (2019). Loneliness is the New Smoking: How Payers and Providers Should Address It. *Managed Healthcare Executive.*

Stroebe, M. S. (2009). Beyond the broken heart: Mental and physical health consequences of losing a loved one. Universiteit Utrecht, 3-26.

Thompson, B. L., & Waltz, J. (2010). Mindfulness and experiential avoidance as predictors of posttraumatic stress disorder avoidance symptom severity. *Journal of Anxiety Disorders, 24*(4), 409–415.

Van der Kolk, B. A. (2014). *The body keeps the score: Brain, mind, and body in the healing of trauma.* New York, NY: Viking Press.

Walker, P. (2013). *Complex PTSD: From surviving to thriving.* Azure Coyote.

Wang, J., Mann, F., Lloyd-Evans, B., Ma, R., & Johnson, S. (2018). Associations between loneliness and perceived social support and outcomes of mental health problems: a systematic review. *BMC Psychiatry, 18*(1), 156.

Ware, B. (2012). *The top five regrets of the dying: A life transformed by the dearly departing.* Carlsbad, Calif: Hay House.

Xu, J., & Roberts, R. E. (2010). The power of positive emotions: It's a matter of life or death – Subjective well-being and longevity over 28 years in a general population. *Health Psychology, 29*(1), 9–19.

Yalom, I. (2008). *From Staring at the Sun: Overcoming the Terror of Death*. San Francisco, CA: Jossey-Bass.

Resources

In the UK:

If you are having a mental health crisis:
Call Samaritans 116-123 (completely free and confidential)
Website: www.samaritans.org.uk

To find a mental health professional in your area:
  Check out https://www.bacp.co.uk/search/Therapists

For information on how to stop child abuse:
  Contact NSPCC
  Phone: 0800 1111 for Hotline to report child abuse
        (24-hour helpline)
  Or 0808 800 5000 for adults concerned about a child
        (24-hour helpline)
  Website: www.nspcc.org.uk

For reporting domestic violence:
  Contact Refuge
  Phone: 0808 2000 247 (24-hour helpline)
  Website: www.refuge.org.uk

For survivors of sexual assault:
    To find your local services phone: 0808 802 9999
        (daily, 12 to 2.30 p.m., 7 to 9.30 p.m.)
    Website: www.rapecrisis.org.uk
    Phone: 0808 168 9111 (24-hour helpline)
    Website: www.victimsupport.org

In the US:

If you are having a mental health crisis:
Call 1-800-273-8255 (available 24/7 free and confidential)
Text: 'HOME' to 741-741 (available 24/7 free and confidential)

If you or a loved one experienced sexual assault:
    Call or message RAINN: 1(800) 656-4673
        (available 24/7 free and confidential)
    Website: https://www.rainn.org

For reporting domestic violence:
    Call 1(800) 799-7233
    Website: https://www.thehotline.org

For information on how to stop child abuse:
    Call 1(800) 422-4453
    Website: https://www.childhelp.org/hotline/

To find a mental health professional in your area:
    Type in your zip code on https://www.psychologytoday.com

Acknowledgements

This work would not have been possible without the constant support of my incredible partner, Dustin. Thank you, honey, for all the hugs and kisses, for always believing in me, and for bringing me coffee in the middle of the night to help me to keep writing.

This book would also not be possible without my amazing editor, Andrew McAleer, whose guidance and faith in me has allowed me to keep writing throughout the years. Andrew, thank you for believing in me when I could not believe in myself. I would also like to thank my agent, Wendy Rohm, for her tireless work to support my writing.

My deepest gratitude to the wonderful editors who worked on this book – Amanda Keats, Una McGovern, and Alison Tulett, thank you for all your wonderful feedback and support. A big thank you to Jill Stoddard and Hilary Graziola for your incredible support and feedback about this book.

To my compassion teachers, Ed Harpin, Thupten Jinpa, Kelly McGonigal, Monica Hanson, Leah Weiss, Margaret Cullen, Kristin Neff, Chris Germer, Michelle Becker, Steve Hickman, thank you for teaching me how to pick up the pieces of my life in a kind and gentle way.

Finally, I would like to express my deepest gratitude to everyone who supported me through this process, especially

my family – Dustin, Hunter, Eddie, Shaye, my mom, Sherry, Rich and Chase – and my writing group – Paxton, Sasha, Shawn.
Thank you all for being wonderful.

Index

abandonment 22, 28, 37, 38, 159
  fear of 71
ability discrimination 87
abuse
  child sexual abuse 64–5
  emotional *see* emotional abuse
  self-abuse, cycle of 142
abuse survivors
  disregard of feelings 66
  fawn response 71
  lack of support 64–5, 66
  re-traumatisation 65
  shaming into acceptance and forgiveness 64, 65, 66
acceptance 63–8
  of assistance 137–46
  avoidance of *see* avoidance
  core value 164
  emotions, permission to feel 65, 67–8, 106
  empowerment and 68
  and enabling, difference between 63–5, 67
  gentle practices 101–11
  Letting the Dog off the Leash Exercise 107–8
  meaning of 2, 63

  mindful 2
  as rebellious act 68
  Valve Exercise 106–7
  what it brings up 86–7
  of yourself as you are 37, 177, 178
acceptance and commitment therapy (ACT) 2
ACT *see* acceptance and commitment therapy
addiction 2, 13, 65, 81, 83
  enabling 65
adrenaline 29, 89
affection, withdrawal of, as punishment 38, 70–1
alcohol 49, 51, 65, 80–3, 167
  emotion-dampening effects 167
  enabling addiction 65
  temporary 'feel good' effect 81, 82
  withdrawal 82–3
alienation 60
Alzheimer's disease 13, 21
ambiguous loss 12–20
  dealing with 14
  physical absence 13
  psychological absence 13
  those affected by 13

types of 13
see also grief
Ana (case study) 64–6
anger 130
  as de-feminising 36, 72
  disapproval of 36, 71–2
  function of 73
  processing 35, 36, 111
  using for your benefit 172
anti-Semitism 56
anxiety 114, 130, 139, 142, 165,
    169, 172, 173
  alcohol and 81
  function of 75
  illusion of control and 172
  physiological reactions 103
  shaming and 1
  social anxiety 50–1
  weakness fallacy 72
anxiety disorders 2
argumentativeness 16
attachments, healthy 37
authentic life 164
avoidance 45–53
  addictive nature of 48, 83
  common behaviours 51–2
  defence mechanism 86, 87
  hiding in a safety zone 48,
    50, 51
  internalised shame and 86
  personal costs of 96
  reinforcement 50, 51, 52
  short-term gain 48

Batman 174
bereavement
  acceptance of 63

feelings of loss 21
lasting impact of 28
self-blame and 16–17, 18–19
see also grief
Beslan hostage crisis 123–4
Black Lives Matter 163
blood pressure 52
boundary setting 86, 147–62,
    164, 173
  aggressive response to 160,
    161
  avoidance of 152
  delaying response to texts,
    calls and emails 158–9
  making requests 152–6
  mental rehearsal exercise
    161
  others' respect for 160, 161
  passive hinting 152
  saying 'no' 152, 159–61
  stepping away from an
    argument 156
  taking a break from a
    person 152, 156–8
breakdowns 83
breaks, taking 141, 174
  from people 152, 156–8
breathing
  breathlessness 116, 165, 166
  shallow 103
'bubble up' visualisation
    exercise 132–3, 141
bullying 31, 32, 47–8, 56,
    58, 87
  fictional experiences of
    58, 59
  self-bullying 87

burnout *see* emotional burnout

cancelling plans 51, 96
cancer 13, 27
carers 132-3
Carrie (case study) 22-3
case studies
  Ana 64-6
  Carrie 22-3
  Chuck 17-20
  Jessica 29-32
  John 50-1
  Julia 119-20
  Laura 39-40
  Olivia 41-2
  Sarah 38
  Vicki 84-6
Chernobyl nuclear disaster 55
chest, tightness in 116
children
  abduction 14
  emotional abuse 38, 70-1
  neglect 37
  sexual abuse 64-5, 110, 187, 188
chronic illness 2, 13, 27, 139
Chuck (case study) 17-20
closure 110
cognitive flashbacks 69-70
comfort behaviours
  comfort eating 51
  see also avoidance
compassion
  compassion cultivation practices 133-4

Compassion for the Monsters exercise 143-6
  self-compassion 118, 131, 133
  see also empathy
core values 2, 164
  honouring 127, 165, 166
coronavirus pandemic 126, 127
cortisol 89, 90
criticism 31, 32
  parental 38, 70, 147
  self-criticism 46, 87, 137, 144, 169
crying 29, 59, 69, 86, 116, 132, 141

death
  deathbed regrets 94-5, 165
  fear of 94, 97
defensiveness 52, 156, 160
depression 2, 13, 15, 16, 29, 36, 65, 82, 114, 131, 139, 142, 169, 172
  function of 73
  illusion of control and 172
  shaming and 1
disability 13, 17-19
  inability to accept 17, 18, 19
disagreements and conflicts 69
  acceptance skills, using 158
  boundary setting 86, 147-62, 164, 173
  empathic communication 158
  urgency response 157, 158, 159
disconnection 49
disgust, function of 73

distraction 51
divorce 13
dizziness 79, 104
dopamine 81, 82
'dragons', battling 88–9, 90

eating disorders 51
emotional abuse
  childhood 38, 70–1
  from others 30, 31, 32, 38,
    56, 110
  self-abuse 16, 37
emotional burnout 130, 131–5
  'bubble up' visualisation
    exercise 132–3
  compassion cultivation
    practices 133–4
  mindfulness practice 133
  recharging your emotional
    battery 131–5
  self-compassion practices
    133
  taking breaks 131–2
emotional disconnection 49
emotional energy 130, 132, 134
emotional flashbacks 69, 70
emotional numbing 130–1
emotional pain
  acknowledging and
    opening up to 33–4,
    40–1, 42, 43, 47, 60, 63, 76,
    86, 90–1, 109–10
  opening and closing
    practice 76–7, 101–2
  rating 102–3
  suppression of 16, 49, 71, 72,
    83–4

weakness fallacy 1, 29, 34,
    59, 71
  see also grief
emotions
  allowing yourself to feel 2,
    59–60, 65, 76, 109, 111,
    132, 141
  'core of the onion' 114, 115
  full spectrum of 45
  functions of 73–6
  letting emotions 'off the
    leash' 108–9
  suppression 1, 2, 36, 49
  see also specific emotions
empathic distress 123–35
  emotional burnout 130,
    131–5
  emotional numbing 130–1
  inability to help 126–7
  moral injury 127, 128, 130
  processing 129
  recharging your emotional
    battery 131–5
empathy 37, 125–6
  empathic communication
    158
  function of 74
  helping others 57, 125–6,
    128, 129–30, 134, 135
  superpower 125
  see also empathic distress
empowerment 2, 29, 68
enabling
  and acceptance, difference
    between 63–5
  shaming into 65, 66
  toxicity 65, 66, 67

unintentional 66, 67
energy
    emotional 130, 132, 134
    release 30–1, 74, 107
explosions, internal 46–7, 72,
    83, 86

families 142
    bereavement 16–17
    family therapy 17
    see also parents
fat-shaming 24, 31, 84–6, 87
fawn response 71, 147
fear
    of abandonment 71
    of death 94, 97
feelings 14, 24, 39, 40, 46, 63,
    84, 111, 141
    see also emotions
fight-or-flight response 52
flashbacks 102, 103, 165
    cognitive 69–70
    emotional 69, 70
food
    eating disorders 51
    fat-shaming and 24, 31,
        84–6
    food allergies 168–9
    mindful eating 85
    relationship with 85–6
foster children 13
friendships 118
frustration 16, 132–3
    function of 74

gamma-aminobutyric acid
    (GABA) 81, 82

gender identity 32, 40, 72, 163
gender-fluid individuals 72
Germer, Chris 76, 133
getting out of bed, struggling
    to 1, 89
ghosting 13
glutamate 81, 82
goals 138, 164
gratitude shaming 23, 27, 36,
    56
grief 11–12, 14–15, 23–4, 114
    ambiguous loss and 14–15
    family therapy 17
    giving yourself permission
        to grieve 24, 63
    'heartbreak' 21, 49
    natural and necessary
        emotion 23, 24
    over other people's pain 28,
        113, 123–5, 126–8
    physical and emotional
        comfort 21–2, 79–80
    processing 12, 15, 24–6
    relationship loss and 9–10,
        11–12, 20, 22–3, 110
    stifling 15
grounding exercise 117–18
guilt
    function of 74
    guilt trips 66, 149, 150

Halloween 93–4
happiness/joy
    function of 74
    physiological reactions
        103
hate, function of 74

healing 12, 45–6, 88, 89–90
  mental health day, taking
      115–16, 141
  taking time to 88, 91
  see also acceptance; social
      support
heart, racing 52, 103, 104, 165–6
'heartbreak' 21, 49
helping others 57, 125–6, 128,
      129–30, 134, 135
heroes 19, 167
  fictional 61, 141–2, 174–5
  origin stories 55, 61–2
  personal 61
heroic pose 166
homeostasis 82
homophobia 24, 87, 127
hopefulness, function of 74
hopelessness 131
  function of 75
human survival needs 37
humiliation, public 56, 57
hydration 141

illusion of control 15–16, 18,
      31, 32, 51, 172
immigration 13
imperfection, running away
      from 94
indifference, apparent 130
infertility 13, 14
infidelity 10, 11, 13, 24
  blaming others for 30
intergenerational trauma 87
internal monsters 142
  Compassion for the
      Monsters exercise 143–6

intrusive thoughts 83, 106,
      117
irritability 16, 130
  function of 75
isolation 16

jealousy/envy, function of 75
Jessica (case study) 29–32
job loss 13
John (case study) 50–1
journaling 3
Julia (case study) 119–20

kindness
  experiencing 87–8
  self-kindness 118, 131, 133

Laura (case study) 39–40
Letting the Dog off the Leash
      Exercise 107–8
loneliness 33, 49, 60
  fictional experiences of
      59
lying 11, 149–50

mental health day, taking
      115–16, 141
mental health stigmatisation
      31, 32
#MeToo movement 163
migraines 27, 55, 83, 139
mind traps 18, 33, 36
mindfulness 2, 133, 141
  mindful eating 85
miscarriage 13, 14, 40
misogyny 87, 127
mobile phones 139

moral injury 127, 128, 130
moral values 127
motivation, lack of 172-3

Narrative Exposure Therapy
    (NET) 120
natural disasters 13, 124
Neff, Kristin 76, 133
neurotransmitters 81, 82
Newton's law of physics 28
9/11 124, 128
non-binary individuals 72
'not good enough' thoughts
    142, 177

obsessive compulsive
    disorder (OCD) 29-30, 31,
    32, 83
obstacles and setbacks
  motivation, lack of 172-3
  normal and expected 167,
    168, 170, 171
  overcoming 167-75
  shame and 169, 170
  unhelpful coping
    behaviours 168
  using for personal growth
    171, 174
OCD *see* obsessive compulsive
    disorder
Olivia (case study) 41-2
oppression 38, 46, 68, 72
  avoidance behaviours and
    83
  fictional experiences of 58,
    59
  internalised 37, 46, 65

origin stories 55-7, 58, 60-1
  becoming a prisoner of 59
  heroes in 58, 61-2
  writing down 60-2
the other 38
over-cleaning 51
overachievers 137, 159
oversleeping 52
overwhelmed feeling,
    function of 75
overworking 52
oxygen mask, metaphorical
    131
oxytocin 20-1, 126, 133

pain, physical
  acknowledging 40
  chronic 2, 105, 139
  managing the experience
    of 104-5
  resistance behaviours 105
  sensations, focusing on
    104-5
  see also emotional pain
pandemics 124, 126, 127
panic attacks 29, 41, 56-7, 65,
    79-80, 83, 114, 150
  physiological symptoms
    103-4
parents
  emotionally abusive 38, 70-1
  relationships with 34-5,
    147-51
people-pleasing 52, 57, 71, 94
  fawn response 71, 147
perfectionism 51, 94, 96, 144,
    159

Phoenix
    awakening 165
    Phoenix moment 42–3,
        178–80
physical comfort 21–2, 80, 126
positivity, toxic 2, 14, 23, 27,
        35, 56, 155
post-traumatic stress
        disorder (PTSD) 2, 13, 15,
        64, 127, 128
power posing 166
prejudice 24, 32, 40, 58, 124
    see also specific types of
present, being fully in the
        95–6
    grounding exercise 117–18
primal scream 71, 124
procrastination 51, 96, 137
productivity and
        achievement 95, 137–8
progress, linear model of 170
PTSD *see* post-traumatic
        stress disorder
purpose, sense of 179

racing thoughts 104, 105–6
    externalising 105–6
    recording 105–6
racism 24, 39, 87, 124, 127, 129,
        134
rebirth experience 121
recharging your emotional
        battery 131–5, 139,
        161
regrets 94–5, 96, 165
rejection 37, 38, 71, 144
relationships

boundary setting 86, 147–
        62, 164, 173
    conflict in 69
    emotionally abusive 30, 31,
        32, 110
    grieving over 11–12
    infidelity 10, 11
    loss of 9–10, 11–12, 20, 22–3,
        110
    parental 34–5, 147–51
    self-blaming narratives 23
resilience 29, 126, 131
    building 168
resources 187–8

sadness, weakness fallacy 72
safety zone, hiding in 48, 50,
        51
Sarah (case study) 38
saying 'no' 152, 159–60
self-abuse, cycle of 142
self-acceptance 37, 177, 178
self-blaming 16–17, 18, 23, 51
self-criticism 46, 87, 137, 144,
        169
self-exploration 2
self-kindness and compassion
        118, 131, 133
self-oppression 37, 46, 65
self-shaming 15–16, 17, 32–3, 37,
        39, 57, 64, 85, 86, 169, 177
self-worth 84, 95
serotonin 169
setbacks
    meaning of 167
    see also obstacles and
        setbacks

sexism 24
sexual assault 28, 64, 67, 110, 114–15, 124, 188
sexual orientation 32, 40, 163
shakiness 29, 116
shame
  anxiety/depression and 1
  body-related 24, 31, 84–6, 87, 169
  function of 73
  gratitude shaming 23, 27, 36, 56
  internalised 15–16, 17, 32–3, 37, 39, 57, 64, 85, 86, 169, 177
  public humiliation 56, 57
short temper 16
slut shaming 24
smoking 51
social anxiety 50–1
social injustices 124–5, 129, 134
social media use 52
social ostracism 56, 58
social support 21–2, 33–4, 37
  acceptance of 137–46
  physical comfort 21–2, 80, 126
  sidekicks 142
  Spoon Theory 139, 140–1
  support groups 33–4
  therapy 34–6, 118
  willingness to ask for 118, 138
Spoon Theory 139, 140–1, 151
Star Trek 72
stomach discomfort 83, 103, 104, 116, 169

Storm (*X-Men* character) 58
stress hormones 89
stuck, feeling 27–8, 33, 36, 42
substance abuse 15, 65
suffering
  acknowledging 48
  healing 45–6
  inevitability of 45
  others' suffering 28, 113, 123–5, 126–8
  weakness fallacy 1, 60
  see also emotional pain; pain, physical; trauma
suicidal thoughts and feelings 48, 49, 65, 102, 114, 131
Superman 141–2
support groups 33–4
surprise, function of 76
survival mode 38, 113–14
sweating 104, 108

terrorism 123–4, 126
texts, calls and emails, delaying response to 158–9
therapy 34–6, 118
  family therapy 17
  prejudice against 34–5
Time Travel Exercise 120–1
timeline of your life 118–19
to-do lists 94, 137–8
transphobia 24, 127
trauma
  grounding exercise 117–18
  intergenerational 87
  intrusive thoughts 117
  naming it 115

others' trauma 28, 113,
123–5, 126–8
'peeling the onion' process
113–21
physiological symptoms
116–17
processing 2, 106, 113, 115
re-traumatisation 65
reaching out to someone 118
suppressing 31
survival mode 113–14
Time Travel Exercise 120–1
writing out your memory
116
see also emotional pain;
grief; healing; suffering

unhealthy coping
mechanisms see
avoidance
urgency response 157, 158, 159

values, core 2, 164, 165, 166
Valve Exercise 106–7
Vicki (case study) 84–6
violence 24, 110, 115, 187, 188
voice, finding your 163–6
core values, honouring 164,
165
stepping outside the box
163
willingness to use your
voice 163
vulnerability, function of 76

Ware, Bronnie 94
weakness fallacy 1, 29, 34, 59,
60, 71, 72

X-Men films 19, 58–9

Yalom, Dr Irvin 94